To Rafic

With many good wishes

Margot

The German-born author came to London in 1962. She got married the same year and immediately moved to Hong Kong with her Chinese husband. When after six years she returned to London, she soon separated from her husband. Becoming a student again, she embarked on a study course of German literature at the University of London. It was during her Master's degree course that she began to write poetry again and to take up teaching as a career. Her publications include two books of German poetry published in Aachen, Germany and *Transforming the Moment*, a book of poems and prayers published by Matthew James Publishing, England.

The author's website can be found at
www.margritdahm.com

With this book I would like to express my gratitude to all those who have helped me to become more truly myself.

Margrit Dahm

WHEN THE HEART BREAKS ITS SILENCE

A True Story of
Loss and Redemption

AUSTIN MACAULEY
PUBLISHERS LTD.

A CIP catalogue record for this title is available from the British Library.

ISBN 9781786123169 (Paperback)
ISBN 9781786123176 (Hardback)
ISBN 9781786123183 (eBook)

www.austinmacauley.com

First Published (2016)
Austin Macauley Publishers Ltd.
25 Canada Square
Canary Wharf
London
E14 5LQ

Chapter One

It mostly appeared to me while I was growing up that I had been born into a strange and rather bizarre family. If reincarnation really existed, so I said to myself, I had obviously made a choice which was neither prudent nor clever.

There was my father, tall and – as my mother would occasionally admit when she was in a good mood – handsome, considerate and kind, and he was liked and respected by everyone. His was a thoughtful and reflective nature: he liked to ponder on things – on issues raised in the family, on expected and unexpected events, on ideas and people's opinions… and when he was in a relaxed mood, he was always ready for a good conversation or sometimes a game of chess. But such moments were rare as he had to work hard to make a living and to provide a fairly comfortable lifestyle for his family.

My mother believed in the beauty of nature, in 'sing a song and all will be well,' in tidiness and strict rules when it came to cleanliness in the house and getting up in the morning. Her flowers on the large balcony were a real picture of opulence and colour, and she took great pride in showing them to people who came to visit. She was prudent and thrifty when it came to money matters: when my father would have liked to be generous, she instantly reminded him of how much it would cost.

My sister and I had, when we were young, our private lives, or rather, I should say, she had: being the older one, she had invented, as I first thought, a very mysterious code of language when she wanted to communicate with her friends from which I was strictly excluded; but what at first appeared to be shrouded in mystery, soon became – as my inquisitiveness would not give up until I had cracked it – the simplest form of a secret language: simply spell the word and always add after each letter the same short word like for instance 'eerie'; if the first letter was another vowel, it would replace the 'ee' in front – once my curiosity was satisfied, I was not interested in their goings-on anymore.

By the time I was eleven, I had my serious doubts as to being a genuine member of this family. I wondered whether instead, I had not been adopted. I always seemed to be the odd one out, and became known, especially during those critical teenage years, for being stubborn, eccentric and rather elusive:

'You are always so reserved,' I often heard my mother say, 'and carry everything to extremes, just like Aunt Mary.'

I knew that she did not like Aunt Mary very much who was my father's sister. She was a lay sister and was in the habit of sending me religious books from time to time which I always enjoyed reading, but were frowned upon by my mother.

As my reputation grew, shoes soon became a first major issue. I wanted nice dainty ones, the kind I saw on the feet of my friends in school. But I was told they did not last. I had to wear shoes with strong indestructible soles that clearly would last forever.

Eventually, I opted for heels. But when I put them on and everybody got ready for one of those long Sunday walks in the country, I was told to go and change them. As to my mind, heels were the only shoes which suited the dress I was wearing, I chose to stay at home and read my book instead.

What bliss to be alone at last! To have the time and leisure to think and dream, to read and escape into the world of my novel where I could easily identify with at least one of the protagonists and so forget for a while what seemed to me sheer misery and endurance:

I craved for understanding, and yet, received nothing but criticism for my behaviour; I wanted my mother to approve of me, but felt that I was failing her in every possible way; even when I tried to please her, it was never quite good enough; nobody seemed to have time for me, for my awkwardness and inner confusion – so I withdrew into myself, and letting nobody see any more how I felt, I started to keep a diary which became my constant friend and companion until the day when I came home and found my diary lying open on my desk; the lines where I had secretly criticized the atmosphere at home saying how it lacked in loving kindness were thickly underlined in red. I could not believe my eyes.

'But this is private! They should not have opened it!'

I kept on thinking, and at the same time the guilt – just as it was intended – was staring me in the face: how could I have written it!

I closed my diary, and closed it for good. After that, nobody cared to discuss the matter with me when perhaps some good could have come of it. Everybody, including my sister, went about their business. The incident was hushed up – nothing at all was said and I was left to feel that they at least owed me an explanation, if not an apology.

But I had grasped that in order to keep out of harm's way, you had better say nothing. My sister followed this rule all the time, she was the diplomatic one; I could not, however, help voicing my inner rebellion and unhappiness on occasions and was betrayed time and again by my frank and outspoken remarks which would always get me into trouble until, at long last, I was ready to leave home and become independent.

This gave rise to the next big issue. I had finished school and considered going to university in order to study German literature; but when I wanted to discuss the matter at home, it caused a serious stir in the otherwise steady set up of the family. My mother said something about being 'too young' and 'girls get married anyway'. I looked at my father who usually seemed to understand me, but he mentioned the word 'cost' to strike the right balance. My sister who had enjoyed a different education from mine, had set a good example in the family by having become the personal secretary in a company, and so having found a sort of compromise, she kept out of the argument altogether. The outcome of it all was that I was allowed to apply for a college away from home where they trained people in modern languages to become interpreters and translators or commercial correspondents, 'for the future lies in speaking foreign languages' was my mother's final word.

I was good at languages. I even liked them which did not, however, make up for the fact that I would have rather plunged into literature, and the history, roots and origins of language development. But I adjusted, and I soon became interested in translating texts from one language into another and in becoming more adept at speaking them. But this, I quickly realised, also involved a stay abroad. In order to speak the language with a certain degree of fluency, I must arrange for a stay in France at all costs (for French was my major language) before sitting my exam.

And with this intention in mind, I went home for the holidays, but as it should turn out, I disturbed once more the tranquil and complacent peace of family life.

'Can't you be content with finishing your course?' I was asked.

'No,' I answered, 'I shall not be able to pass my exam if I don't improve my oral French.'

'You give us nothing but headaches,' was my mother's comment which made me feel yet again sad and misunderstood when at the same time I saw nothing but plain logic in my argument.

I knew by then that my mother found it difficult to come to terms with the fact that her daughters wanted to fly the nest, but still, I could not see what the problem was this time.

Reluctantly, under the influence of my father who put in a good word for me, she agreed to let me go provided my father drove me there and checked out the family where I was meant to stay as an au pair for six months.

We were finally on the way to Paris and made our way to Fourqueux, a small village outside Paris where we met the parents of the four children I had come to look after. My father made use of his own knowledge of French to chat to the father who I called Monsieur. He led me to the piano where on top of it stood a large photograph displaying four young children and pointing to it, he said:

'Marguerite, vous avez du courage !' Margaret, you have courage!

And it took courage indeed, to look after the two boys and two girls whose age ranged from four to seven. Madame very wisely went out that first day and left me in charge; but she also took me to the local Prisunic store so that my pretty summer frocks could be put away in favour of a pair of blue jeans (which my mother had never approved of).

The children soon came to like me, and I liked them and I treated them with respect and understanding as far as I was capable of doing so at my young age. I was nineteen at the time. I looked after their rooms, washed and mended their clothes and socks, walked the two younger ones to school every morning and fetched them again at lunchtime when they came home for lunch before returning to school.

I spent a lot of time with the cook in the kitchen who took a keen interest in improving my spoken French while I would sip a large cup of leftover cocoa and cream. When friends came to visit and the grown-ups gathered in the large garden which formed part of the back of the house, Monsieur always made sure that I was included.

I was happy in France. Removed from the rigid and narrow pattern of my home and without the reproving look and scrutiny of my mother, I began to feel for the first time that I was a young adult who had a right to have her own views and opinions, but who also had responsibilities. I began to enjoy my newly found freedom.

We lived twelve kilometres away from Paris, and on my free afternoons, I took first the bus, and then the train into Paris, arriving at Gare St. Lazare. I would then take the turning to Boulevard Haussmann and find myself a table in one of the many street cafés there and soak in the ambience around me while watching the passers-by or reading my book and French newspaper.

I also appreciated the efforts the family made to help me mix with people of my own age such as when they introduced me to the son and daughter of friends of theirs who lived nearby. And there was my boyfriend of course, who quickly got the nickname 'le gendarme' because of the dark blue suit he usually wore on these occasions. French policemen are always dressed in dark blue. He was ten years my senior; we had met in the college library and had been going out together for about a year. In his battered little car, he made the journey repeatedly in order to come and see me. He usually got delayed on the way when he had yet another mishap with his car. Then he would ring telling me that he was running late. The whole family got involved every time we were waiting for his arrival, and when he was finally in sight, the children were always the first ones to spot him:

'Marguerite,' they would shout, 'le gendarme, il est arrivé!' He has arrived!

In preparation for a holiday in Brittany in the summer, I went to the big department store Lafayette in Paris, and for the first time, with my own money, without the keen eyes of my mother looking over my shoulder, I bought myself a pair of cotton trousers in soft rose with matching shorts and a jumper in plain beige. I felt so happy and proud!

I never forgot the wonderful time we had in Brittany. We left home when the sun was just rising over the horizon and drove through the wild uninhabited countryside until we finally arrived in Port Manech near Pont Avon where Madame had rented a holiday cottage. I loved the room I was given where, in the evenings, I could listen to the sound of the waves as the cottage was very close to a small beach. Here, we tasted the well-known 'crêpes'- crisp and wafer-thin pancakes from the griddle - accompanied by strong Calvados, a spirit which is distilled from apples, and went for walks on the beach. My boyfriend came to visit me in the same old battered car and I was allowed to take the day off so that we could travel to Brest which, as a port, had been an important strategic point during the Second World War.

When I finally returned to college after seven months, I was not only able to speak French fluently, but I had also come to like the French way of life and had adopted some of those traits which I had found to be so appealing and sympathetic. I had tasted a new slice of life, and it had made me more confident and outgoing, giving me altogether a more positive outlook. This was possible because I had had the good fortune to be around friendly, open-minded and considerate people who allowed me to be what I was: a young woman aspiring to make her way in the world.

Shortly before the time of my exam, my boyfriend's sister who translated French books and who at the time had too much work on, handed one of them on to me, and so, when I had successfully passed my exam I returned home in order to finish the translation there. I quickly realised that this type of work provided the challenge I enjoyed and I therefore began to write letter after letter to countless publishers. But nothing came of it. On each and every occasion I was told that I needed a degree in literature if I wanted to have any chance at all of working in that sector.

I wondered what I could do next. The thought of having to work in an office was troubling me as it was something that had never attracted me very much. I had helped out my father occasionally with running his office at home when he had to go on a trip, and had realised then that this was not how I saw myself earning my living.

When I had finished the translation of the book and it was accepted for publication, I was paid a certain amount of money. I was by then twenty-one years old, it was the year 1962, and it seemed as if my parents had come to the conclusion that they had done their bit. My sister, who was still working as a secretary, had together with the rest of the family settled into a daily routine from which I felt strangely excluded; it felt as though I was standing apart; it also seemed as if I could do now as I pleased as long as I did not ask for my own set of keys in case I wanted to go out, or even perhaps have a night out. But that was well-nigh impossible anyway, for I had no friends to speak of anymore at home, and my boyfriend who lived in another city, would sometimes visit me during the holidays, but these visits always remained brief and short-lived.

I realised I had to do something. As questions about a possible career were never discussed with me in any shape or form, I came up with the idea of moving on to London, and to my surprise, no more objections were raised, no more issues discussed; as I could not get myself to apply for an office job and did not feel confident enough to do anything else, I applied for a mother's help position with a family who lived in Ealing, a suburb in West London.

Chapter Two

London overwhelmed me at first. As I had been raised in a smallish country town in West Germany, I felt utterly lost among the hustle and bustle of Central London and the vast network of the Underground and busses. But I quickly adjusted to my new situation and learned to find my way around as young people always do.

The family, or rather the couple I stayed with could not have been more different from my family in France. The lady of the house was expecting her first baby and wanted someone to look after him/her when he/she was born so that she could return to work. Meanwhile, there was a lot of housework for me to do, and when I had worked hard all morning, I was hungry and ready for my lunch. This took place in the kitchen, most of the time in silence, and it consisted mainly of a few lettuce leaves, perhaps a bit of cooked ham and a slice of bread. I was too polite to ask for more, and so I would find an excuse to go out in the afternoon in order to buy myself some chocolate and biscuits, for there was no afternoon tea. The only decent meal was in the evening when her husband returned from work. After the meal they would retire and go to bed.

This went on for a good while until I realised how lonely and isolated I really felt. I thought of a way out of this predicament and came up with the idea to look for a church nearby and perhaps join a club. After some research I enrolled in 'the Linguist Club' which was situated in Notting Hill Gate. Here people sat in the lounge leisurely sipping tea, or else they were engaged in talks and discussions that took place in different rooms and in the various languages that the club had to offer. I partook in the French conversation class where topics were suggested and a speaker chosen to give a talk which could then be discussed.

I volunteered with the question:' Est-ce que la souffrance est necessaire pour la sagesse?' – Is suffering necessary in order to become wise? The question resonated in me, and I took my time to think about it. I have somehow never forgotten this first deliberation of mine about a subject matter which should turn up later in my life again and again.

My talk was an instant success and raised many questions, and even when the discussion was over, people still came to me and wanted to hear more.

Eventually, I made my way to the snack-bar in the basement where I ordered some coffee and sat down next to another girl. Her name was Eve, and we soon began chatting about London and explaining what had induced us to join the club. In fact, we got on so well together that she invited me to her party which would take place in her boyfriend's apartment. His name was Adam and he was Chinese.

The party was one of those typical get-togethers where you had something to drink and did a bit of dancing. When it was time to go home, one of Adam's friends, also Chinese, offered to take me back to Ealing, and when he asked for my telephone number, I gave it to him nonchalantly not knowing that this simple little gesture would turn my life upside down and completely change its course.

Meanwhile, I continued to visit the Linguist Club, and sometimes someone from the club would accompany me to the nearby underground station. Once it was a tall black man, well-mannered and polite, and then again an American, equally courteous, who told me that he came from a Mormon background. Whenever I let them know that I already had a boyfriend, they always quietly withdrew respecting the reply I had given them.

Chapter Three

It was some weeks later when I received a telephone call.

'Oh yes, of course,' I lied when I was asked whether I could remember him.

'Would you like to have dinner with me?' he asked.

I hesitated, then declined, but when he kept on insisting, I finally gave in and accepted the invitation.

He came to fetch me in his sports car, and as I scarcely knew London, I could not make out where we were going. He finally stopped in a residential area in front of a huge block of flats.

I looked around and asked perplexed: 'Where is the restaurant?'

The penny dropped when we got out of the car and he said matter-of-factly:

'I have prepared dinner at home.'

'Oh, I see,' I said hiding my surprise, remembering that I had been left under the impression that we would have dinner in a restaurant.

When we entered, I could see in the kitchen two large steaks neatly laid out on a wooden board, a bottle of red wine was standing on the side, and French beans in a sieve had been washed and were ready to use.

Seeing the care that had been taken in preparing the meal, I began to relax a little and sat down in the sitting room. He put on some music and made himself busy in the kitchen. Dinner was quickly served, and we chatted and answered questions about our lives in London. I told him that I had a boyfriend, but that we were going through a crisis. He explained that he was a student and that he was in his final year of studying law. I was aware of the fact that I was not particularly keen to get to know him more intimately, and therefore, when it was approaching ten o'clock, I got up and told him that I had to go home.

He also got up, but only to put on some more music telling me that he would drive me back.

'Would you mind if we left now?' I asked politely.

'Why don't you have another glass of wine before we leave,' he suggested while opening a door next to where he was standing and disappearing behind it.

I waited for a while thinking that he would return, but when nothing happened, I finally got up, knocked on the door and opened it.

I found him lying on the bed. I approached him in order to ask him once more to drive me home. But he had other intentions.

What followed was but a play to him – I dimly realised that. For me it was the uncalled for intimacy with someone

I had only just met; but I had yet to learn how to guard against such forthright and rash behaviour, and I therefore remember it all as something quite distasteful and performed in rather a hurry. Then he got up immediately and said:

'I'll drive you home now. This flat is not really mine; it belongs to a friend of mine. I only borrowed it for the evening as I live in a rented room in Swiss Cottage.'

When I was ready to leave, I experienced, as I crossed the entrance, a whole array of mixed feelings. I felt humiliated, cheated, sad and abused.

Someone to whom I had shown my trust when he invited me in had broken all codes of decent behaviour. But in order to focus on the present moment, I had to detach myself from what I was feeling. At least I wanted to make sure that I got back safely, and not much was said on the way back.

The next day, I had made up my mind that should he ring again, I would tell him that I did not want to see him anymore.

But he didn't ring. Instead, he turned up on my doorstep and asked me out for a coffee. If my parents had taught me anything, it was always to be honest and polite.

So I agreed to have the cup of coffee with him bearing in mind, however, what I wanted to say to him. I chose my words very carefully when I had to tell him that I saw no future in our relationship. He seemed so confident that this was the beginning of a beautiful friendship.

He quickly responded to the statement I made by admitting that, as it was the summer vacation for the university students, all his friends had gone back to Hong Kong and that he felt very lonely in London. He pleaded with me in earnest asking me to give him another chance.

The word 'lonely' had immediately struck a chord in me and out of sincerely felt empathy I let myself be persuaded to meet again. He arranged for us to go to the cinema and see 'Dr. No,' the first of the James Bond films with Sean Connery in the title role; then he got tickets for a performance of 'Swan Lake' in the Royal Albert Hall; he invited me to a small intimate Italian restaurant where we could bring our own bottle of wine, and I also met him in the Chinese restaurant where he used to work as a waiter during the holidays and where he would serve me a meal teaching me at the same time how to use chopsticks. I began to enjoy going out with him in the evenings thus getting to know some of London's attractions; but it was usually quite late by the time he drove me back to Ealing. This continued for a while until I was finally called into the sitting room and was told by the couple that I was no longer welcome in their house.

As I did not have the kind of relationship with my mother which could have allowed me to count on her support, it never once occurred to me that I could have simply returned home. Instead I asked my new friend whether he could put me up for a short while, and he agreed to let me stay until I had decided what I wanted to do.

I was now sharing his room with him in Swiss Cottage, not knowing what I should do next. The decision was made for me. A month after I had moved in with him I found out that I was pregnant and I had now to think about the implications this would have for me.

'You have three options,' the doctor I consulted told me, 'you can have an abortion, have the baby adopted or keep the baby.'

It did not take me long to decide that there was only one option for me and that was to have the baby. But how was I going to earn my living? I replied to two advertisements in the Evening Standard and went for interviews one of which was in a music shop where I would be some sort of girl Friday; another one was in a publishing house where I would have similar duties.

I had yet to take the first step on the ladder of the job market, and I hesitated. It never went beyond the stage of an interview. So I confronted instead the difficult task of telling my parents in a letter what had happened. As far as they were concerned, I was still with my boyfriend who my mother had never really approved of. But what would she have to say when she heard that I was pregnant, that the father of the baby was a young man from Hong Kong and that my boyfriend had been told that it was over?

Meanwhile, the prospective father had been told, and he had sought the advice of his friends who had returned to London for the next term. And so, when he came back one night, he pronounced matter-of-factly:

'You'd better have a good sleep tonight because we are going to visit your parents tomorrow. I am going to marry you.'

I was dumbfounded, and for the first time I felt for him something like sympathy born out of solidarity.

Though I had not really been aware of it, the fact that we were sharing his room had naturally drawn us closer together.

At the same time, however, I still held on to the thought that I might have my baby at home and that I could stay there for the time being, and when I received a letter written by my father where he simply said:

'Such being the case, you had better come home,'

I felt almost certain that a solution could be found to my problem which would suit everybody.

Chapter Four

We set off, as he had said, in his car early next morning, and his friend who had helped him to make up his mind about his proposal came along as well. They found it wiser and more convenient for them to stop half way and to put me on the train: I had to face my parents on my own.

I felt apprehensive, but not altogether distraught and I was looking forward to seeing my family again.

It was my sister who came to fetch me from the station saying:

'You must expect the worst.'

All at once, I woke up from my dream and I knew that having lived away for several weeks, I had forgotten what it was like to 'come home'.

My reception was very formal and cold. No one wanted to break the ice until we finally sat down at the dinner table, and my mother began to blame me openly for 'having brought shame on the family,' and even hinted that I could have had an abortion. I tried to explain, but she kept on interrupting me.

My father tried to intervene by saying:

'Let her speak!'

But it was of no use. The general atmosphere remained tense, unforgiving and strained. My parents went to bed that evening and not a kind word had been said to me.

I knew then that another future lay ahead of me, and it did not lie in the bosom of my family. When therefore my father suggested next morning that, under the circumstances, I'd better stay with them, I firmly said almost surprising myself:

'He has proposed marriage and I am going to accept.'

After yet another gruelling day, my 'fiancé' turned up at their doorstep and introduced himself – to my utter amazement, my mother took an instant liking to him when she learned that we were going to be married. My future husband at first took it for granted that I would like to have my family around me when we got married, but it was soon conveniently decided that we should return to London in order to have the ceremony there.

During those crucial days and hours, I was quite incapable of gathering my thoughts or feeling anything at all except the strong sense of rejection I had experienced when I came under fire from my mother, quite unjustly so, I felt. Never once did she care to find out what had really happened.

Had she been able to listen and been more understanding, I could have told her that I was not sure at all about marrying him; at the same time, I would have felt less guilty which in turn would have allowed me to have the clarity and presence of mind to know what I really wanted to do.

I was badly in need of somebody I could confide in, and my sister must have felt my need to have someone near to talk to, for on the last evening together when we were alone in our room which we still shared, she expressed her reservation about marrying somebody who, after all, came from a different culture and who must therefore have different values and attitudes.

I knew she was right and I knew that it was a gamble, but I said to her:

'I can only try, and try I must.'

As to my future husband, I was not given the time and opportunity to ask myself what he must have felt or what he made of the family he was marrying into though he seemed to get on fine with my mother. There was little time for any reflections or musings. I only knew that, after the three days were over, he, too, was happy to return to London.

When we were back in Swiss Cottage, we made the necessary preparations for our wedding. His two closest friends would be our witnesses, and we would celebrate the day by having lunch in an Italian restaurant in Soho.

On the morning of our wedding, I put on the black suit with the frilly white blouse which had been provided by my mother for me, and in order to make it look a little bit more like a wedding outfit, I had treated myself to a pair of black satin shoes.

We stepped in and out of the Registrar Office in Swiss Cottage in a matter of minutes. I held a tiny little bouquet in my hands, and when our two witnesses took a picture in front of the entrance, it all seemed rather unreal because my heart which during all this time I had never once been allowed to consult, was not really in it. I had to look down to the tips of my shoes in order to think:

'This is my wedding.'

I vaguely remember that while we were having lunch and the three boys were engaged in conversation, my thoughts finally caught up with reality: I was able to say to myself quietly:

'I am married now,' and I looked at my husband by my side as if, by looking at him, I could read what the future would hold for us.

My thoughts turned to the boyfriend I had left behind and whose proposal I had rejected. He came to see me while I was staying with my parents saying:

'I'll marry you with the baby.'

Instead, I had decided that marrying the real father would provide the best future for my baby.

When we finally went home that afternoon, it was his turn now to worry about what members of his own family might have to say, and this time there was no turning back: it was a fait accompli – he was married to a 'white woman' and they wanted to meet her…

He gave me a few lessons in preparation of this big event. We went to see a film which was shot in Hong Kong, and he gave me some more practice in using chopsticks – for he, too, had received the answer:

'Come back to Hong Kong and bring your newly-wed wife with you.'

Another long talk took place between him and his friends where his future was discussed. He had considered the possibility of moving to San Francisco where friends of his could perhaps help him to find some suitable work.

But it was generally decided that, for the time being at least, the best plan of action was to respect the wishes of his parents and to leave for Hong Kong.

Air tickets were bought and we were set to leave for Hong Kong in six weeks' time. There really was no respite. We had known each other for three months, and without being allowed to really get to know each other, we were now confronted with the prospect of moving to the Far East and would have to face together all the difficulties which such a big cultural change would entail.

Did we care enough for each other to meet such a challenge? Would we have the strength to grow into our new roles, to stand united in front of any adversity we had yet to brave, and above all, would our relationship be allowed to deepen and expand and develop into something real and meaningful?

At the time, these questions were never clearly formulated or expressed. They only remained, while the daily preparations and events took over, a vague hesitation and uncertain apprehension stored away somewhere in the background, and by the time we boarded the plane, were almost forgotten.

Chapter Five

There were early warning signs that our marriage might be built on weak foundations. On our way to Hong Kong we stopped over in Athens. My husband had a friend there and he wanted to go and see him. After our arrival we checked into a hotel. It was early evening. When we had settled in, he said to me:

'Why don't you take a rest while I will get in touch with my friend?' and left the room.

As I was indeed feeling tired, I soon fell into a restless sleep from which I woke when I heard a noise in the room. I switched on the light and saw my husband just having returned. I looked at the clock. It was four in the morning.

I noticed that he had drunk quite a lot as he was not quite steady on his feet, and the words came pouring out of his mouth:

'I am sorry, so sorry! I was just going to explore Athens a bit, but there was this woman, and she took me to her flat...so sorry...'

I received the news with a strange kind of placid acceptance at first: at least he seemed to feel quite guilty about it. Somehow I knew that this was not the last time I would have to listen to such a confession. I could not go back to sleep after this. I lay awake wondering what my future was really going to be like, what it could hold for me when my husband who had spoken of this trip as being our honeymoon, was unfaithful at the first opportunity that had presented itself. I felt very lonely and subdued that first night on our way to Hong Kong, and this feeling of isolation would not leave me and continued to cast its shadow over the day which followed: I could not shake off the memory of the events of the previous night.

We went out to do some sightseeing after breakfast. We climbed up to the Acropolis where we took some pictures, had lunch in a Greek restaurant together with his friend, and left Athens later that day. Last night's embarrassment was neatly put away and not mentioned anymore.

Our next stop was Bangkok, my first experience with the glamour and glitter of the Far East. I took in the scene of the poor districts at the outskirts of the city with their primitive huts and poorly dressed men and women, and countless children lining the streets. In their rags they held out their unwashed little hands begging the passers-by for money and waving at the same time at our taxi which was taking us towards the centre of the city. It came to stop in front of a splendid looking hotel: its wide portals were flanked by two enormous golden lions in a crouching position, and the entrance hall itself was equally bombastic and elaborately adorned with gilded ornaments – the contrast between two such different worlds was startling.

After a short rest and a change of clothes, we went to meet a family friend and his wife who had invited us to have dinner with them in a Chinese restaurant. Being the guest of honour, I sat next to the host who saw to it that my bowl was constantly filled with morsels of the various dishes which, one by one, were continuously being served.

33

As it had been past my dinner time and as the food was really very tasty, I began to eat with a hearty appetite, but when the plates of food still kept on coming and my bowl was still being filled, I had to force myself to finish it so as not to be impolite.

When we finally returned to our hotel, we sat for a little while on the adjoining balcony, and I can honestly say that I have never again felt so full in my life. Those poor people living in poorly assembled huts who had to make do with scraps of rice and vegetables came back into my mind, and yet, I mused, they had not appeared to be unhappy.

When we went inside, my husband pointed to a particular fruit lying in the bowl on the table, a fruit which I had never seen before.

'You must try this,' he said to me and cut the fruit open. Its flesh had the colour of butternut squash, but was soft to the touch.

It tasted delicious and I was told that it was papaya.

Early the next morning, we boarded the plane for the last time. The next stop was our final destination: Hong Kong – which means translated 'fragrant harbour'. As we approached the built-up area of Hong Kong Island, the plane began to descend sharply, and as we were flying over Kowloon which is part of the mainland, we almost seemed to touch the rooftops of the houses. This was necessary, I was told, because the runway was built out into the sea and had to be approached from a very low angle. It was quite an extraordinary and alarming sight.

When we had landed, my husband peeped out of the window and must have spotted members of his family awaiting us on the terrace of the airport. He turned round briskly, and fear was written all over his face. He said:

'I don't want to get out!' and I realised at this moment, that he, too, was afraid of having to face his family and whatever was awaiting us outside this plane which was our last connection with a world we were rapidly leaving behind.

We left the plane and were joined by the family at the gates.

I was introduced: there was the eldest brother and his wife from mainland China, the second eldest who was yet unmarried, his youngest brother who flew with an airline, and his youngest sister who was still a schoolgirl. His two elder sisters, I was told, lived in America.

Everybody shook hands and gave me a big welcoming smile, and to my relief, everybody spoke English. The youngest brother who was in his early twenties, engaged me immediately in a conversation, and I soon felt that I had found a friend in him. The eldest brother and his wife were a bit more formal, slightly more reserved, but polite and friendly, and the youngest treated me at once quite naturally as her equal.

The driver was waiting for us outside and drove us to a restaurant where we were soon seated at one of the many big round tables, and the conversation began to flow freely; often forgetting that I was there, they chatted away in Cantonese. It felt strange to be so far away from everything I had ever known, and having to listen to the sounds of a language I could not understand intensified my impression that I had entered a world which was totally foreign to me and which I did not belong to.

After our lunch, we crossed the harbour on the car ferry, and I saw for the first time the impressive panorama of Hong Kong island with its high-rise buildings being overshadowed in the background by the 'peak,' the highest point of the island. The harbour itself looked busy: there were plenty of colourful, old-fashioned and shabby-looking Chinese junks mingling cheerfully with elegant and luxurious private yachts and other larger-sized motorboats and vessels.

When we were once more in the large American limousine, we left the centre soon behind, passed the racecourse in Happy Valley and stopped in front of an enormous bright red gate. The gate was opened by an amah, one of the servants, and the car parked in the courtyard.

I guess, we were both a bit nervous when we got out of the car because the moment had come when I would meet my mother-in-law. But she seemed friendly enough: apart from the fact that she did not speak a word of English, we took to each other as you do when you cannot rely on words, but only on gestures and expressions.

Our luggage was taken out of the car and brought upstairs where we were given a bedroom with an adjoining bathroom on the second floor of this very large house. Apart from another bedroom which was occupied by the eldest brother, his wife and little boy, there was also on this upper floor a generous, but sparsely furnished living room which led to a very large terrace outside.

When I was finally left alone in the bedroom while the rest of the family gathered together downstairs, I was suddenly overcome by the impact and novelty of the many strange and overpowering impressions and events as they had impressed themselves so vividly on my mind and which wanted to be assimilated in such a desperately short length of time. In a moment of acutely felt estrangement from my new environment I fell down on the bed and sobbed my heart out. I felt anxious, alone and desperately homesick for anything, anything at all that was in the slightest bit familiar.

But just at this moment, my husband entered the room and seeing me in tears, he came over and comforted me in the nicest possible way: he was the link now between this and the world as I had known it. – After a few minutes, I was able to compose myself and was soon ready to have my first dinner at the large round dining table downstairs on the ground floor being surrounded by my new family. A variety of meat and vegetable dishes were placed on the inner rotating disk of the table, and everybody helped themselves to rice which stood on a tray nearby. The conversation was in Cantonese, but as I was sitting next to my husband, I could put in the odd English word. I thanked him silently for the fact that he had given me sufficient practice in using chopsticks as I now had to do as everyone else did, and this was by no means easy.

Adjoining the dining area were the kitchen and the servants' quarters. The kitchen was entirely the domain of the cook and some amahs who were standing by to help her. A passage way in the courtyard connected kitchen and servants' quarters. Here, the rooms were like little cells in a beehive, just big enough to contain a narrow plank bed and a small side table. The rooms were windowless as the back of the house faced the high and steep wall of a rocky mountain.

The dining area as such was part of a wide open lounge with pieces of Chinese furniture and a large comfortable couch. The centrepiece was a beautifully carved cabinet on top of which stood the three large Buddha-like statues representing longevity, prosperity and happiness. There were also three bedrooms on the ground floor occupied by my mother-in-law, the youngest brother Horace and the youngest sister Mandy with her two Pekinese dogs. Apart from that, there was a smaller compact room which one could call a study and where I would later give language lessons for a while.

The first floor would later be occupied by the second eldest brother when he finally got married and had two little girls and a son.

The whole house was so spacious that despite the large number of sons, daughters and a growing number of grandchildren who gradually filled the house, it never felt crowded in any way. There seemed to be plenty of room and space for everyone.

I went to bed that first night knowing that I had passed the initial test and I told myself that it could only get easier as time went by.

Chapter Six

The unsettling experience of the last few weeks and months was quickly replaced by the regularity that followed. As it always does, life regained its usual heartbeat in a newly established routine.

My husband joined the family business and went to the office every day, while his two elder brothers who were trained engineers worked in the family's factory in Aberdeen. I spent a lot of time in our bedroom reading and writing. I had brought some of my own books, but I also wanted to know more about how to care for a baby and obtained a copy of the book written by the then leading American paediatrician Dr. Spock which was recommended to me by my doctor who had been trained in America.

A bell was attached at the top of the backstairs which could be rung from the kitchen down below. The sound of the bell always signalled that lunch was ready and that I should come downstairs. Often it was only my mother-in-law and Yso, my older sister-in-law who were having lunch at home, and when I later discovered a delicatessen shop in the central district where I could buy a variety of breads and cold cuts, I quite often stayed upstairs to enjoy a lunch I was more accustomed to, and nobody seemed to mind.

But dinners remained a family affair where everybody came together downstairs.

In the beginning, I had the idea to explore the neighbourhood a bit more by taking a stroll outside, and so one afternoon, when the sun was shining, I left the big red gate behind me and followed the road leading me downhill. But I had not walked very far when I was pursued by a gang of children who seemed to shout something. Unnerved by the noise and spectacle, I turned and went back. When I mentioned it in the evening to my husband, he explained that those children always call out 'white devil woman' when they see a European face, and I was advised not to repeat my escapade; but it also meant that I could not do a simple thing like going for a walk to soak in the atmosphere of my new surroundings.

A teacher was employed who came to the house twice a week to teach me Cantonese, and I told him that I also wanted to learn how to write the characters. So I began the painstaking process of learning a language which had no associations at all with any other language I knew. I enjoyed practising the characters, and my teacher showed me occasionally how the abstraction of the modern character could be traced back to a time when its representation was still of a pictorial nature. He showed me for instance how the character for 'moon' could easily become a crescent moon, if you curved the outlines a bit, and I was fascinated by it.

I also came up with idea that I in turn could teach as well by giving English or French lessons at home, and sure enough, somebody wanted to polish up his French. The lessons took place in the study behind closed doors, but only a few weeks had gone by when my husband told me that his mother did not approve of the fact that I was alone in the room with a strange man, and the lessons were discontinued. I was shocked at first, but on reflection I had to admit to myself that this was not the first time I had come across a different attitude towards women and that this incident fitted the picture as it began to take shape in my mind. But it was yet a vague nondescript notion which would only become clearer in the course of time.

My mother-in-law and Yso, the wife of the eldest brother, were often driven to the Central District to go shopping and have tea somewhere: not English afternoon tea, but Chinese tea – 'iam tsa' which means 'drink tea' translated – where large quantities of green tea were drunk and all kinds of steamed dumplings, both savoury and sweet, were being served. It is particularly popular as a lunch time treat. So sometimes the bell would ring and I was asked whether I would like to come along, but I must confess that I mostly preferred to stay in my own company. I was not in the habit of going shopping very much, and by then I had begun again to feel somewhat the odd one out which this time, of course, I was in every sense of the word. So the occasions where I joined them on their outings remained few and far between.

In the evenings, the house came to life when the men returned from work. Dinner was served and there would be much chatting and joking going on while we ate; but it was always in Chinese, and so, most of the time, I was limited to being the silent onlooker unless I asked the odd question.

After the evening meal, the boys and also my sisters-in-law often came together to play mahjong where, again, I remained only a spectator. I knew that my mother-in-law frequently played the game for large sums of money, and when I approached my husband asking him to teach me the rules of the game, he said, obviously referring to his mother:

'The reason why I didn't want to marry a Chinese girl was precisely because they do nothing but play mahjong and go shopping'.

But surely, he must have known by then that I did not enjoy gambling of any kind while, it is true, the Chinese on the whole are only too prone to it, and so was my husband. Of course, there was some truth in his statement, particularly among the richer families, and his mother was certainly part of this upper class circle where life was led as a life of leisure; but it would have greatly helped my social skills to feel more included when the young ones were having fun. No one, however, ever asked me to join in and the game was never explained to me. It seemed an established fact that I would be sitting somewhere nearby watching them playing or retire to our bedroom to do some reading.

On Sundays, his father came to join us for lunch. He spoke some English, and when I met him for the first time, I liked him instantly. Then and in future he would always have a kind word for me. He spent the rest of the week with his other family which consisted of his 'mistress' as she was referred to, and the two children from this second 'marriage'. Sunday lunch was therefore a more elaborate affair, and quite often friends or relatives who came to visit were invited to share the meal.

Twice a year the entire family clan with aunts and uncles, cousins, nieces and nephews would assemble in the house, and we all had to pay our respects to the ancestors. There was on the wall in the living room a large-sized painting of the parents of my father-in-law. Underneath stood a table.

A special meal would be prepared in the kitchen, and when all the dishes were ready to be served, they were placed on the table beneath the picture. The family gathered round. First, one after the other, starting with the eldest and finishing with the youngest member of the family, stepped forward to bow in front of it; then all of us counted in Cantonese one, two, three, and together, we made once more our bow to the couple in the painting. It was all done in a good-humoured kind of way. There was nothing solemn about it. The food then went back to the kitchen to be heated up before we all sat down to eat.

As the Chinese do not follow the lunar calendar, Chinese New Year is usually in January. The loud noise of firecrackers could be heard everywhere, and people were shouting:

'Kung Hei Fah Choi!' – 'Happy New Year!'

The younger ones received little red envelopes containing 'lai chi' – 'lucky money' from the older members of the family, and there was in the house a lot of coming and going and to-ing and fro-ing throughout the day.

And then there were the dinner parties, not at home, but in a restaurant. If it was a big occasion, an entire floor would be hired usually consisting of two large rooms filled with enormous round tables which seated about ten people each. People would arrive in the afternoon and start to play mahjong until it was time for dinner to be served. And it was not uncommon that men and women were segregated; I would then find myself surrounded by Chinese ladies in their finest attire adorned with diamonds and jewels. On my arrival in Hong Kong, I had been given a diamond bracelet and brooch by my mother-in-law so as to fit in socially when I had to attend these large dinner-parties; when I was thus seated among other young women, polite conversation took place, questions were asked and respectfully

43

answered, but I never felt that anyone of them was really interested in getting to know me better.

'Perhaps it is me,' I often wondered, but it never happened that talking between us became a bit more spontaneous or natural. It never went beyond the rather meaningless phrases of formal courtesy, and they quite often simply forgot about me and chatted away in Cantonese. The progress I made in understanding and speaking the language was slow. I would pick up a common phrase here and there and would say the odd word, but it still was really an undiscovered country for me.

The food was always delicious, and course after course would be served, the final dish usually consisting of a sweet hot soup made of almonds followed by orange segments which finished off the meal. Drinks consisted mostly of brandy or whisky which was diluted with water or ginger ale, and as the guests had been drinking since the afternoon, the level of noise increased rapidly, until the fruit on the table signalled the end of the evening and instantaneously, without further ado, everybody got up to say their good-byes.

The male members of the family who had hosted the dinner, lined up in the entrance hall to shake hands with each of the parting guests.

It was on these occasions that I came to realise that my husband did not hold his drink very well and got quite drunk almost every time. In his drunken state, he could display unpleasant bouts of jealousy which could be easily aroused by very minor incidents such as a simple smile or friendly word which, unthinkingly, I might have exchanged with another man. These scenes occurred almost every time after such a big dinner and were always totally unprovoked and completely groundless as, I am sure, he knew.

Something in me told me that these sudden outbursts where I was accused every time of having done wrong for no apparent reason reflected his real attitude towards women: his English education would then come into conflict with a much more deep-seated idea about what a wife should or should not do. His wife was not allowed to be his equal and must be kept in her place.

I knew practically nothing about his childhood, but I can well imagine that he did not grow up in a happy family. When his father left his mother and had come to some sort of arrangement with her, she blamed the other woman entirely for the break-up, and she looked for the necessary support in her sons in order to maintain her claim. Her sons were still young at the time. In the case of my husband, I can therefore assume that the image he had of women had been influenced accordingly, and as we women in the West are used to being in many ways equal to men and enjoy independence, his English education and his Chinese upbringing might well have clashed in this instance. This could have resulted in some underlying fear which compelled him to make sure at all cost that he always remained in control. It also made it impossible for him to admit even the smallest of mistakes on his part or to reveal his true feelings, for that matter.

This is the way how I view it now looking back. But at the time, young as I was, I lacked the necessary insight to make sense of it all and began to feel that I was gradually losing my identity.

It was November when we had arrived in Hong Kong, and the weather was pleasantly cool, but warm enough to leave the windows open. I enjoyed the spring-like temperatures, and I soon needed some more light maternity wear. A tailor was called in and I was allowed to choose some nice cotton fabrics to suit my taste. Up till now, it had been an easy pregnancy for me with no morning sickness or any other symptoms, and as the baby began to grow inside me, I grew accustomed to my condition. The regular lifestyle we had adopted since our arrival in Hong Kong had given me, against all the odds, a feeling of stability and security, and there were times when I felt almost happy.

My senses were sharpened by the many unusual smells and sounds surrounding me. At night, with the windows open, I could hear very distinctly the loud chirping of the crickets populating the tough gorse-like bushes which covered the steep barren mountain rocks outside, and this was accompanied by the regular rattling of mahjong pieces when one game was over and the next one about to begin – a sound which I came to associate so closely with Hong Kong as it was audible in every street and every district, especially during those hot and sticky summer nights when for those who did not enjoy the luxury of air-conditioning, the windows remained permanently open.

From the kitchens rose the smell of ginger and aromatic spices so typical in Chinese cooking. It all became very familiar to me, something which I so badly needed in order to make sense of my life. I started to write letters to my family at home where I shared some of my experiences with them, but I always made sure that they contained nothing that could have upset or alarmed them. I was overjoyed when I received a parcel from them containing lots of baby clothes and some toys, and I thanked them enthusiastically; for every little gesture, every little sign from the old familiar world was received with more than a grateful heart.

I sometimes watched my husband in the early evening hours when having come home from the office, he would fly his kites from the terrace on the upper floor where the aim of the game was to cut the strings of other kites sailing in the sky, and for me it meant that I was watching a side to him which had been hitherto unknown to me. It was refreshing to see him spending some time on a leisure activity which seemed to give him some pleasure and which, most likely, was something he had learned when he was a boy.

On another occasion, he announced that he would take me out. We went down to the harbour, just the two of us which was rare enough. We went to the poorer district where the boat people lived and worked, and to my surprise he urged me to step into one of these small boats. We were seated comfortably, as far as the cramped conditions would allow, and left the quay where the majority of the junks were anchored.

The boat stopped when we were a distance away from the shore, and sitting in the familiar crouching position which seems so effortless to the Chinese people, the woman in the boat began to prepare a meal by using freshly caught fish and prawns. The rice was cooked, the vegetables fried, and we enjoyed a most delicious meal that could not have been better in the most expensive restaurant. To our amusement, a toilet roll was passed round for us to clean hands and mouth.

My husband was in such a relaxed and happy mood as I had seldom witnessed it before; we chatted and laughed and enjoyed ourselves as any happy young couple would, and at that moment I felt quite reassured and was certain that, though we might have had a bumpy ride and a turbulent beginning, things would turn out to be alright for us after all.

Chapter Seven

After a very short spring in February when the trees in our road flowered and produced a kind of bright red blossom which I had never seen anywhere else, the temperatures began to climb sharply. By March the humidity had increased to such a degree that it felt uncomfortable. The air-conditioners were switched on at night. It took some time to get used to falling asleep in the cool air while windows were tightly shut and the only sound you could hear was the humming of the air-conditioner.

By the time April arrived I was sweating profusely during the day, and the discomfort I experienced then in this humid heat would never leave me while I lived in Hong Kong.

I was in the last month of my pregnancy, and when the month of May was nearly at an end, I woke up one night with the pangs of childbirth. It was four o'clock in the morning when we arrived at the near-by hospital. At daybreak my doctor came to examine me and said that there was still a long way to go. The day went by and the contractions came regularly now, and still I was told that I was not yet ready to be delivered. The doctor went home that night saying that he would be back in the morning.

When morning came, I was utterly exhausted and my husband was told that there might be complications. However, they took me into the operating theatre and the baby was successfully delivered with the help of forceps. When I was finally back in my room with my husband by my side, I held the baby, whose head had been bandaged, in my arms for the first time – I was exultant. My husband was overjoyed: he was the proud father of a son. Such a moment is never forgotten.

But I have equally not forgotten that, as the nurses in the hospital hardly spoke any English, arrangements had been made for my husband to return to the hospital after work and to spend the night on a provisional bed made up for him next to mine. These few days seemed almost dreamlike: we experienced a closeness which would never be repeated.

My mother-in-law came to see me together with her eldest son Ygoh, and he translated for me what she wanted to tell me. She explained:

'I take care of every first born son of every son of mine'.

On many occasions, I had watched Ygoh's little boy being spoilt by his grandmother in every possible way, and quietly, but firmly I had made up my mind that this would not be the case should I give birth to a boy, that I as his mother would be there to look after him, and that his grandmother would have to play second fiddle.

After three days I was allowed to go home, but for a week, a nurse came every morning to help me bathe the baby. I quickly learned from her how to handle him, and when the week was over, I felt confident that I was able to manage on my own. A cot was put up in our bedroom, and so began my life as a mother. I put into practice everything I had learned from reading my book on babies and childcare, and when therefore I was given a baby amah who was supposed to take care of him, I told my husband that I didn't need her as I wanted to look after him myself.

After two months, he began to sleep through the night, and a normal rhythm was quickly established.

I was adventurous in my approach to feeding him and introduced bit by bit freshly squeezed carrot and orange juice and small spoonfuls of baby food.

By the time he was three months old, he had not only tasted apple sauce, but also mashed vegetables, and pureed meat or chicken. I felt happy and fulfilled.

And so was his father. We took pictures of our son, and I started an album with all those little cheering comments underneath. We took him out to the beach and let him have a first taste of the sea, and I caused a big stir when I put him out on the balcony in the early morning sun dressed only in a nappy and a little vest.

The amahs came and stood round him and couldn't believe their eyes. For them, babies were meant to be wrapped in blankets and thick layers of clothes. My mother-in-law who was obliged to watch from a distance, was certainly not convinced that this was the way to look after a baby. My sister-in-law consulted me asking how I had managed to make him sleep through the night when his little cousin of three years old was still waking up regularly.

Every little piece of news was shared, everything observed and taken notice of: his first smile, his first sitting up in his cot while nibbling on a rusk, his first crawl and standing up ready to take his first step.

But by then I knew I was pregnant again and I asked myself how we would manage with one bedroom and two babies. With Mandy, the youngest in the family, being the interpreter I put the question to my mother-in-law; I had to plead with her as she seemed to be reluctant to help at first.

It had come to her ears, she explained, that we wanted to move out – was this true, she asked; to which I replied quite truthfully that I knew nothing about this; she seemed pleased with my answer; for when a few days had passed, the small room next to ours was cleared out, and when the second baby was born, it became the nursery for our little son.

My second pregnancy was as easy as the first one had been. I ate healthily and only put on the weight I was supposed to put on. I took out again the list of names and studied it: if it was another boy…if it was a girl…

By then, I was really settled and was leading the life which Hong Kong and its surroundings allowed me to have, and for the first time, I got acquainted with a girl who, like me, had met her Chinese husband in London and was now living in Hong Kong. It felt good to be together with someone who shared a similar experience and with whom I could exchange views and opinions and compare lifestyle decisions.

Time went by, and our little daughter was born a year after our son. The birth was an easy one, but when I was home again, I began to feel the responsibility of having to look after a toddler and a newborn baby: I had my hands full now, but at least I was able to concentrate on the children as everything else was taken care of.

Thankfully, my husband had always considered it a temporary solution to live under the same roof as his mother, and so the time had come when without my knowledge a flat had been bought in a newly developed area, and he took me to see it. I was pleasantly surprised when we entered a very spacious living area affording a wonderful view over the sea from the two very large windows. There was the master bedroom ensuite and two other bedrooms, and the kitchen had an adjoining small room for a servant. A staircase led to the roof terrace as we were on the top floor, and this would be ideal for the children's play area. It was, however, quite remote, removed from any traffic, shops or public transport. I would have to rely on the family's driver as before if I wanted to get out at all. But as the flat had already been purchased, and I was never consulted, I would have to deal with this problem when we moved in.

I was looking forward to having at last a place of our own, and a carpenter was asked to build different parts of furniture for us according to my own design as they were then no furniture shops in Hong Kong. I developed a colour scheme for curtains and carpets, particularly for the spacious living room, but also for the children's bedrooms, and it all went to plan.

Two years after our arrival, we finally moved out of the big family house into our own apartment. I had awaited this move with great anticipation as by leaving behind the dominant and constant presence of my mother-in-law and the rest of his family, I was looking forward to a time now where I was finally allowed to create the kind of life that I wanted my family to have, and this also included spending more intimate moments with my husband. During the past two years I was compelled to make many sacrifices and adjustments and had learned to renounce my wish to be alone with him so as to balance out the many occasions where I had felt outnumbered. My expectations were therefore high when at last, the time had come for us to be free of too close a supervision, of too much control and family pressure.

Chapter Eight

At first, it all seemed nothing but a change for the better. We were a young family and could now enjoy our privacy. The children enjoyed their new freedom of having a room each where they could play, and there was the upstairs terrace where there was yet more space to run about. I had a sandpit and a seesaw installed and there was also a little plastic swimming-pool. My husband had now his own car which took him to the office and back. I arranged my books on the newly made bookshelves and had my own desk where I could do my writing and my Chinese homework.

I could dedicate more time to improving my skills as a cook as I had a modern kitchen now. Sunday luncheons remained a family affair, but otherwise we could develop and create our own lifestyle.

It was suggested that I should be given a live-in amah who could keep our home clean and tidy, and perhaps do a bit of cooking. But when she arrived, I was soon uncomfortably aware of her continued presence in so confined a space, and when she started to carry my little baby daughter in a sling on her back, I decided to let her go. For there was the problem: I was always at home as I had no means to go out. As she did not speak any English, the communication between us was minimal, and I also felt that my privacy had been compromised. I was acutely aware of the fact that she spent all her free time – and there was plenty of it – in her tiny little box room next to the kitchen with only a bed inside. Perhaps to her, this was what she was used to, but I had been brought up with the notion that we are all equal and worthy of being fairly treated, no matter what kind of work we do, and so I found this situation quite unacceptable. I had to explain this to my husband, and she was dismissed soon after. When she had left us, I began to establish a regular routine where I would do a little housework in the morning, do my writing and homework while the children had a nap and then spend the afternoons with them on the roof terrace.

By then, I had two European friends, both young mothers with Chinese husbands who would come and see me from time to time bringing their young children along with them.

I was keen to become a better cook and studied cookery books which I had brought along in order to experiment with different flavours and recipes.

But whatever I served in the evening, it somehow never seemed to be good enough for my husband. I got the impression that, without ever saying so, he preferred his Chinese food to anything that I cooked, but it instilled in me the idea that I was a bad cook, and it took me many years before I was able to discover that I not only enjoyed cooking, but that I was also good at it.

When the children were a little older, I would ask the family driver sometimes to come and pick me up, and he would drive me to the market where I now enjoyed to haggle for the best price in Cantonese when I bought my meat and vegetables.

Quite soon after our move, however, a subtle change took place that would soon become a regular feature in our life. It happened less and less that my husband was home in time for dinner. At first, I would keep the food warm, put the children to bed and wait for him to come home. But it usually got later and later, and when he eventually arrived, he was half drunk and went straight to bed. When I approached him the following morning, I was told that he had gone to the Malaysian Club with a colleague from the office, and I took it that this was going to be the occasional, if not frequent drink after office hours. When it happened more and more often, however, I confronted him one morning before he left for the office, but he flew into one of his sudden tempers and slammed the door behind him.

Communication came to a standstill between us. We were only together when we had Sunday lunch at his mother's or when we had a social engagement and went out.

Socialising is an integral part of the life in Hong Kong. Friends and family invite you out and you invite them back in return.

There are the expensive and sophisticated restaurants in the big hotels, and there are, of course, the many Chinese restaurants for a less formal affair. After dinner at a hotel the evening was often rounded off with a drink at the bar or at one of the city's night-clubs. We had a small circle of friends by then, both European and Chinese, with whom we were in regular contact.

Taking all this into account, I had to admit that we had practically no home life to speak of. It was always me and the children. The occasions when I could ask the driver to take us to the beach which meant an outing for us, were few and far between. Whenever there was no engagement, I was mostly on my own in the evenings, as my husband continued to prefer spending his time with his chums from the office and was hardly seen at home.

As the family business expanded, he also began to go away more often, first exclusively to countries in the Far East, but later he also travelled to the Middle East. I accompanied him on two of his trips while the children were looked after by their grandmother. The first trip took us to Taipei in Taiwan where, coming from the airport, you see nothing but the vast expanse of the plains which were divided up into paddy fields. Singapore which we visited on our second trip together, seemed so much greener compared to Hong Kong because residential streets were here lined with houses which had well-kept gardens back and front, a luxury which Hong Kong's built-up areas could ill afford.

These two short-lived diversions from my daily routine could not hide the fact, however, that I was beginning to feel a void inside me which would not leave me anymore. It was the vague feeling of being, despite my motherhood, somehow unfulfilled, a longing for something that I could not quite understand or grasp yet. I knew I craved for communication, for a meaningful conversation, an exchange with someone close to me, and the obvious person who was meant to be close to me, was my husband. But when I put it to him one Sunday that we hardly ever spoke, talked, chatted or laughed together anymore, he simply replied:

'I don't know what you are talking about' –

The problem did not exist for him.

I also became aware of the fact that in all the time we had been together, I had not received any sign of affection, be it a kiss or an embrace – oddly enough I had somehow never called this into question, but had, without fully realising it, missed a more obvious expression of tenderness and love.

Such sudden and notable insights, however, were quickly swallowed up again by the usual daily humdrum events and occurrences – and in an attempt of securing my escape route, one which had proven to be effective every time, I returned to my books, my faithful companions. I started to read the writings of Lao Tzu and studied his philosophy, and I continued to read books which dealt with particular areas in education such as the Montessori Method or the aims of Pestalozzi's kindergarten. But I could never discuss these ideas with anyone as the conversation in the company of our friends generally consisted only of small talk, and there was no one who I could have called my closest and dearest friend.

Culturally, Hong Kong had then very little to offer which could enrich one's intellectual or emotional life. There were no theatres, concert halls or art exhibitions, only the cinemas. Even bookshops where one could buy classics of world literature or books on specialist topics were as good as non-existent. The little bookshops which were commonly seen in the Central district offered only Chinese books, their windows openly displaying the 'red book' of Mao.

And so began the period of time for me when I felt inwardly more and more alone and emotionally starved for something real, something which did not yet lend itself to being defined or named, but which began to be present in me like an intangible, but unmistakable ache that was never far off, always lurking in the background, consistently waiting to be addressed.

The only chance I had to articulate my feelings in some ways, was in the letters I wrote to an old friend of mine whom I still knew from my college days, and to my former form teacher who was a Dominican nun and with whom I still maintained a close relationship. Here, I tried to express as best I could what was weighing me down, and I was always looking forward to their replies.

I continued to focus my attention on the upbringing of my children, and so, when we were able to celebrate our first Christmas in our new home, I wanted to make it a special occasion. Among the Chinese population in Hong Kong the majority of which have either Buddhist or Confucian beliefs and customs, Christmas is nothing more than the remnant of the old colonial past. It lacks meaning. But I set about finding a pine tree with its long needles and then decorating it the best way I could. It seemed strange to make preparations for Christmas when the weather outside was spring-like and warm, the cloudless, azure blue sky being of an immaculate glowing radiance. I bought little presents and made some cookies. A Christmas parcel arrived from home which also contained a tape with Christmas carols. To see the enchantment in their eyes when the children were finally allowed into the living room, was sufficient reward for my efforts.

When the year came to a close, the children were now two and one year old, and we had lived in Hong Kong for three years. My husband announced that early in the spring, we would go and visit my parents and take a holiday in Switzerland. This prospect revived my spirits, and I was very much looking forward to being back on familiar ground.

Chapter Nine

With both the children being so young, the journey back to Europe turned out to be very cumbersome and tiring. My parents came to fetch us from the airport, but we were not able yet to respond adequately to their eager 'hellos' and animated greetings as we were thoroughly worn out and exhausted from looking after an overexcited little boy and an overtired little girl.

When we arrived at home, it became immediately clear that my mother had excelled herself in providing absolutely everything needed for two young children.

There was not only a baby cot, but even a walker and a playpen. She told me that she had been able to borrow most of it from friends. Both my parents were overjoyed to meet their grandchildren at long last, and my sister who was still unmarried, played her role as their auntie amicably and lovingly. The children were so excited to be in a new and unfamiliar place where everything was worthy of being explored. This was especially so for my lively little son who was curious just about everything, and it did not take him long before he had his grandfather on all fours so that he could have a ride on his back. It was a happy reunion. Just like the first time when my husband was introduced to my family, he seemed somewhat different in their presence, more approachable, attentive and generally more amenable.

The shadows which had kept us apart for quite a long time now, seemed to lift, and there were warm feelings and good cheer all around us.

I began to relax. I listened to the music and old-familiar tunes coming from the radio; at first I was just glad to hear them again; but quite suddenly, the outer wall of resistance which had prevailed for so long began to crumble and my heart gave way to a wave of nostalgia which I had never been allowed to acknowledge or express; tears came to my eyes, when already I heard the forbidding voice of my mother who was sitting nearby:

'What are crying about now? Stop at once!'

And I was instantly reminded that in our family, emotions were mostly hidden and covered over, sometimes even deeply buried in the unconscious. You were expected to deal with them in your own private, if inadequate way. You were entitled to express moments of joy and good cheer, but as to the realm of heartfelt sadness, grief or sorrow, the doors were kept tightly shut in order not to appear weak-willed or spineless as one might cause a stir by arousing sympathy or, even worse, pity. The wide scale of legitimate and genuine feelings and emotions as they exist in the human psyche was simply wished away – outwardly, they did not exist at all.

I would have liked so much to confide in her at that moment, for the music had touched me to the core; I needed a friendly soul so badly, a sympathetic ear who would have listened to what I had to say. But it was not to be: I had to be the happily married woman my mother wanted me to be, and my husband became the devoted father and husband they wanted to see in him. Thus pretence and truthfulness, illusion and reality were strangely muddled and mixed while we were staying with them, and everything which did not fit into the general atmosphere of good-humoured congeniality, was kept out of reach, with the result that we all got on fairly well together with the children being the centre of attention.

Our little daughter was applauded for taking her first steps while everyone was watching, and our son came bursting into the room one morning exclaiming excitedly:

'It's snowing! It's snowing!'

And, indeed, snowflakes were beginning to cover the pavements outside. It was a thrilling sight for the children as they had never seen any snow before, and my sister volunteered straight away to look for the old abandoned sledge in the cellar. As soon as everyone was dressed, they ventured out and had their first tobogganing experience. They came back red-cheeked and full of energy telling everybody who wanted to hear it, how great it had been.

When the snow began to melt away after a few days, we were ready to say our good-byes in order to board the plane again which would take us to Geneva. The children had thoroughly enjoyed their stay with their grandparents, and as to us grown-ups, we seemed at least to have struck a note where we could honestly say: it had been a pleasant stay. My parents as well as my sister had relished their new roles, but by the time our visit was over, were equally glad to see us go.

Chapter Ten

In Geneva, we checked into a hotel by the lake. That night, we all went to bed early in order to do some sightseeing the following morning.

I woke up while everybody was still fast asleep. I got up, got dressed and quietly left the room. When I stepped outside, the morning bustle had not yet begun. The air was fresh, cool and scented, and as the sun was making its way upward, there was still a tranquil feel in everything around me. I let myself be guided by the road I had taken, and was soon climbing the gentle slope of a cobbled street. I was happy to be on my own and so able to enjoy and take in keenly what I saw and observed. I took a deep breath realising that this was my first walk since I had left Europe, and I could savour it on this sunny, but chilly morning in spring, in a climate that suited me so much better.

When I came nearer to the top of the hill, I saw to my right the tower of a church, and when I was close enough, I could hear some music coming from within.

I opened the heavy door and entered. I was at once surrounded by the most exquisite sounds in an otherwise empty church. The softly vibrating tones of a violin were responding to the iridescent tunes of the piano creating a harmony together which had an ethereal quality to it and which reverberated throughout the nave of the old and dimly lit church. I sat quietly in one of the back benches and let the music take hold of me. I experienced an inner serenity and peace which penetrated me and reinstated itself like an old forgotten friend. All longing, all nostalgia were fused together in an overpowering feeling which instilled in me a first glimpse of the true meaning of faith, hope and love. When I finally got up in order to return to the hotel, I knew that this was the missing link in my life which I had been searching for.

I found my family having breakfast in the breakfast room and making plans for the day, and it took me a while before I was able to tune in and play my part again. But something stayed with me throughout the day, as if I had been nourished for the first time in a long time with the kind of food which had been absent for so long.

When we were back in Hong Kong after this first return to Europe, I took up my life again as before and on the surface, I forgot again about the experience I had in Geneva; but somehow something remained alive in me and seemed to help me when dealing with the different duties and responsibilities or coping with emotional upsets. It should be another three years before the big change would come and we could move back to London.

Chapter Eleven

My husband began to travel more than ever before. He visited not only the Middle East now, but went as far as Africa where he had set up business relations with the Sudan and other countries.

On one such an occasion, when he had gone to Beirut, I received the message:

'Pack your suitcase and come.'

I was surprised as this had never happened before, and I was quite stunned as I was expected to leave everything and be on my way, for as he said, time was of the essence. So I rang up the airline, packed a small case and told the children that they were going to spend some time with their grandmother. The driver came to fetch us and I was on my way.

I landed in Beirut at daybreak, and the sun had only just risen, when the hotel coach passed through the quiet and empty streets of the outlying suburbs where hardly anyone was out and about yet apart from the white-clad figure of a man now and then who was drawing his cart behind him.

In the hotel, I was seen to what I believed was the room of my husband, but when I entered, I realised that it was an entire suite he had at his disposal. He was in very good spirits and wanted to show me the rest of the apartment.

When he opened the door to a second bedroom, I came face to face with my sister whom he had asked to join us for a few days. The surprise was complete. This impulsive gesture and his spontaneity enabled us to enjoy our time in Beirut, and I willingly nurtured the thought that he could still be kind and considerate.

When my sister had left, he went about his business while I was driven round the city by one of his business associates who was a Palestinian. Beirut was then still a beautiful city. Its immaculate whitewashed buildings formed a stark contrast to the deep blue sky and the deep blue sea having the snowy mountains as a backdrop. My companion demonstrated to me how, as soon as you leave the city behind, the car had to climb steeply into the mountains, and it was not long before we could step outside and see the remnants of clumps of ice and snow lying by the wayside. The view from there showed us the peaceful picture of an elegant city yet totally in tune with its environment.

This very accommodating and knowledgeable Palestinian also took us under his wings when it came to food. He took us to a Lebanese restaurant. The meal consisted of many different little dishes placed on the table all at once, all of them beautifully spiced and flavoured, while the fragrant, slightly bitter coffee tasting of cardamom was poured from a certain height into the small cups. The coffee pots themselves were made of brass and their long curved spouts had the shape of oversized beaks upside down.

This trip was a truly welcome interruption from the daily routine in Hong Kong which after a while becomes so easily claustrophobic because of its dense population and the lack of space from which there was no escape. I appreciated it that my husband, on this occasion, had shown real insight, sensitivity and consideration when he gave me the chance to experience something new, combining it at the same time with the visit of a member of my family which had come as a total surprise – it was altogether a gesture which would then give us back, for a brief stretch of time at least, the positive notion that we belonged together and could be there for each other.

The children were now of an age where they could attend a kindergarten, and my mother-in-law insisted that my son should be enrolled in a nursery where only Mandarin was spoken; for my father-in-law was the patron of the school. When I accompanied my husband one morning as he drove him to the school on his way to the office, I saw my son going up the stairs and entering the room looking totally lost and forlorn as he was standing among the other children. I burst into tears and said:

'You must get him out of there!'

He did leave the school, and we soon found a nice kindergarten run by an English lady where both our children could learn English as well as Cantonese. They were happy there.

As the children were now away from home for part of the day, the opportunity arose for me to get involved in a school project together with two other ladies one of whom was a trained teacher. We envisaged a school where children could have a proper English education which would help them to ease their way into the English school system in England when their parents were going to be repatriated, but where they could also acquire a knowledge of Chinese. We were able to rent three school rooms and started to divide the children up into different age groups. It turned out to be the beginning of a school which would soon grow in size and which is still flourishing to this day.

With all these various activities going on, my life appeared, outwardly at least, to be a bit more varied now, but at home things were far from showing real signs of improvement on a more long-term basis. More and more often it became apparent that we lived different lives that only coincided when we went out which was very frequently the case. What I had expected to happen when we had moved out of the family house, had not materialized. I missed those moments of togetherness which couples share, where feelings for each other can be refreshed and renewed, and I missed an atmosphere in which thoughts and emotions could be openly expressed and communicated. This in turn would have created an environment where closeness and mutual trust could be cultivated; but this can only come about if both partners are willing to share what they think and feel. This never happened, and I was often under the impression that, while the whole experience had accelerated my development as a person, he had never really moved out of his shell as he hardly ever let me see what must have been his inner world. For this reason, I mostly felt like the older one, the one who had to cope and put up with things when, in fact, he was my senior by several years; at the same time I was not allowed to be his equal; but to be on equal terms seemed for me the essential ingredient in a relationship which was true both in intent and meaning.

The thought of leaving Hong Kong and returning to Europe together with my children was never far from my mind. But I knew that I had not the financial means to support such an idea. When it was therefore decided by the family that the company should open an office in London and that my husband should be in charge of it, I received the news with great joy and relief. Perhaps this was the chance for us to start afresh and to begin a life which was more suitable for us both and for us as a family. Away from the glamour and shallowness of Hong Kong and back in England where he had received most of his education and where we could therefore feel both at home, things might change for the better between us and draw us closer together as a family. When I therefore began to pack suitcase after suitcase, I was looking forward to a new chapter in our life together.

Chapter Twelve

We arrived at Heathrow airport on a cold and frosty morning in March 1968 and drove straight to the Royal Garden Hotel in Kensington High Street where we were given a suite consisting of two bedrooms and a living space. At first, there was the joyful acknowledgement that we were back in London and in a nice hotel with Kensington Gardens right next door where the children could run around freely. Our first stroll through the park soon proved to us how cold it really was. The bitter northerly wind that blew round our ears went right through our ill-suited clothing, and the pond was covered with a thin layer of ice.

Adjustments had to be made, winter clothes bought, and, of course, there was the thought of finding suitable long-term accommodation. My husband set about getting in touch with estate agents while I had to keep the children amused. But searching for a furnished flat turned out to be more difficult than expected, and as the days went by and this question became more and more pressing, my husband grew more and more impatient and ill-tempered which in turn made the children more restless and irritable. I was walking on a tightrope, it seemed, in order to keep spirits up and keep some sort of a peaceful situation among us. He began to tell me off for minute errors, and though it made me feel more and more incompetent, I kept my composure just so that things would not get any worse.

Eventually, after three or four weeks, he was able to rent a smallish, compact flat on the ground floor of a big block of flats off the Edgware Road, and as soon as we were settled there, he left on a business trip to the Sudan. Meanwhile, I tried to get used to our new accommodation where the children shared a small bedroom next to ours. I explored the area: for I was now able to do my own shopping, to take the children out, to be among people – all the things that mothers do. I also looked into schools as the children would be ready to start school in the autumn, and I found a nice private preparatory school nearby. For the first time in my married life, I could have a daily routine which included going out and moving about freely.

On one occasion, when the children were asleep in the afternoon, I decided to take a short walk as the park was so close by. It began to rain. I did not mind the rain: I welcomed it. When I followed the pathway which led me further into the park, I could smell the air scented with the freshness of grass and soil, I could see the old trees and bushes around me, I took in the people passing me by, and suddenly the thought finally became a reality and I understood:

'I am back in Europe, I am back in London!'

In this quiet moment, I could at last make a mental note of what had happened, and this gave way to a feeling which I could only describe as a feeling of absolute bliss and elation. The last time I had experienced a similar feeling was when, after the long and difficult birth of my son, I was finally holding him in my arms for the first time. This time, too, I silently thanked God for having brought me back to a world I could relate to and connect with. When I went back to my children that day, my spirit felt strengthened by the hope that the future could now be faced in a better way.

Chapter Thirteen

After six months, a larger unfurnished flat on the third floor became available in the same block, and my husband rented it immediately. The children, now five and four years old, had just begun to go to the school I had chosen for them, and I could now dedicate myself to the task of making this flat our home.

After a lot of searching, my husband had found two empty rooms in a building in Upper Regent Street which would serve him as his new office, and together with an old friend whom he had contacted, set about painting and decorating the two rooms and finding suitable equipment.

He told me that I was free to go to Harrods and visit the furnishing department there. With the help of one of their assistants, a colour scheme was soon decided on for the different rooms of the flat. We had to furnish three bedrooms and a large l-shaped living/dining area. As I seemed to have a flair for decorating, I was able to proceed fairly quickly. Wallpapers, carpets and curtains were selected followed by carefully chosen items of modern furniture. I went for warm, muted tones rather than the bold patterns and strong colours as they were the vogue in the sixties.

After two months, we were ready to move in. The children's room in its cheerful colours had a double bunk which they could share, and so the extra bedroom could be kept as a spare room.

When the office was ready to be used, I volunteered to see to the correspondence as I had now the time to do so. I sat in what was the reception room, while the two men had a desk each in the adjacent room. But there was as yet very little for them to do, and in order to make up for what must have been quite a boring day at the office, they would come home with cans of beer and start drinking.

I mostly tried to ignore it, but could not help noticing that his friend and now business associate had become a fixture in our home during the week. At week-ends, my husband was now mostly absorbed in the horse races on television and placed his bets accordingly. This kept him busy all afternoon at the expense of everything else. As before, there was very little interchange between us, and he continued to show his displeasure about minor things occurring in the home:

'Stupid, you are so stupid!'

Became his constant remark branding me with the kind of label that stuck to me like strong and unpleasant goo.

I had the feeling that I could not please him in any way, and this continued in the office where everything I tried to do did not seem right at all. I tried to improve my office skills by attending a correspondence course which lasted for six weeks and which I finished with an excellent result.

But the general atmosphere in the office, I felt acutely, was very often tense, as the two men had too little to do to keep them busy and occupied, and so, oddly enough, I became the pawn who could be constantly criticised and subtly abused. I came to the conclusion that my intention to help and to make myself useful had failed. So I let them get on with their affairs and employ someone else instead.

However, my husband soon intensified his travelling abroad in order to open up new markets and set up new business relations. He was good at his job, and business began to flourish. As a result of this prosperity and expansion in business, I was given a Chinese housekeeper to do the housework.

But as always, I was not consulted about something that after all, affected my life considerably, but instead the decision was made for me and I was faced with a fait accompli. She moved in with us and was given the spare room.

It would turn out to be a very strange set up indeed. There was the housekeeper who, when my husband was away, would seek my company in the evenings to have a chat, and there was my husband's friend who seemed to spend more time in our home rather than in his own. At the same time, both of them were far too familiar with the rows and arguments which had fast become common place between my husband and myself when he was at home. The situation was quite intolerable, but could not be discussed with him at all.

In my desperation, I took a decision which in hindsight brings to light only too clearly how unhappy I must have felt. In order to shake him out of his complacency and make him realise that life could not continue in this way, I decided to go away for a limited period of time.

As before, it did not occur to me to seek shelter at my parents' home, but instead I rented a room in another part of London which also had a kitchenette and shower. I let the housekeeper have my contact number and address and told her to look after the children for me until my return.

I mostly spent my time reading the kind of books which I had neither the time nor leisure to read at home. My old friend from college with whom I still corresponded, sent me a French book written by G.I. Gurdjieff, a teacher of a particular school of thought and philosophy. When I sat down to read the book, it had a very strong and lasting impact on me. I became conscious again of my desire to get in touch with something deeper within myself, something that contained a certain wholesomeness and profundity which was absent from my life, and it awakened in me the wish to seek a way where this something could be realised. The question: 'Why am I here?' and 'Who am I?' stood now before me with an absolute clarity and urgency, and I knew that, if I wanted to find the answer to this question, I would have to find people who searched in a similar fashion.

But first, I must deal with my family, and at long last, I decided that it was time to go and see my parents; perhaps the occasion would arise where I could discuss my problems with them.

It was a welcome change for me to be at home again and to be surrounded by all the things I had grown up with.

One afternoon, I tried to approach the subject of my marriage with my mother. I tried to explain how difficult it had become to make sense of it all and that I might eventually decide to end the marriage.

She said:

'But you can make yourself a comfortable life! And what about the children?'

I said:

'I have thought about that, too. But if there are constant arguments and friction in the family, it might be better for the children if the parents are not together anymore.'

This was all that was said about it. She did not seem or maybe did not want to understand how unhappy I had become. Perhaps I had not articulated it plainly enough. In any case the outcome of it was that my parents then endeavoured to bring us together again: my husband was informed and told that I was staying with them and was asked if he and the children could come and join me here at their home.

I naturally was overjoyed when I was reunited with the children, and my husband said that he had learned his lesson and made promise after promise that things would be different in future.

On our return to London, he dismissed the housekeeper and also his friend and business associate. He booked a holiday for us which he called 'a second honeymoon' where we would go and explore the Norwegian fjords while he had arranged for the children to stay in a 'kinderheim' in the Austrian Alps.

I would rather have stayed with the children who no doubt had been affected by the whole ordeal, too, and I took all this activity and the seemingly big change for the better with a pinch of salt not being entirely convinced that it could last. But as always, it was his decision and his decision alone.

At the same time, I wondered, knowing that he was of an impulsive and volatile temper, whether he was at all able to persevere with his good intentions which on the spur of the moment might even have been sincere. However, only the future would tell whether anything would come of it at all.

Chapter Fourteen

The cruise along the fjords was breath-taking and wonderful. But during the entire stay on the boat I felt oddly numbed and restrained, and I vaguely realised that it was mostly caused by the apparent unresponsiveness and lack of interest on my husband's part who did not seem to see the majestic beauty surrounding us nor did he want to communicate any enthusiasm, but was instead mainly concerned and occupied with his physical welfare. Once more, it was so very obvious how little we had in common, how little we could share, and it left me bereft of any enjoyment. I was forced again to withdraw into myself and with a feeling of sadness I resigned myself to the inevitable. I also missed the children, and I therefore felt hardly alive at all on this trip and could not appreciate and admire what would otherwise have been a glorious and impressive experience.

When we disembarked, he hired a car which would take us to our destination, a hotel situated on the shores of a small lake. En route, he complained about the road which was narrow and winding its way through undergrowth and woodland. He seemed rather anxious and nervous.

The idyllic sight of the small hotel by the lake which could have been cut out of a picture book, worked its magic, however, and he relaxed when he was able to park the car in the courtyard. The room was comfortable and welcoming, and we were told that dinner would be a buffet where everybody could help themselves to as much as they wanted. We unpacked and he suggested, as it was only late afternoon, to take one of the rowing boats out on the lake. Our mood lifted, and while sitting in the boat, I watched him do the rowing and tried my hand at a drawing to capture the scenery of our immediate surroundings. – Was it possible that he was really making an honest effort to please us both rather than only himself? Could there be a 'we' rather than just 'he' and 'I'? – As it were, he seemed to have enjoyed this little excursion, and we returned to the hotel full of good humour and a healthy appetite.

The food was delicious. There were delicacies like lobster and fresh salmon, salmon trout and succulent prawns. There was a variety of meat, too, to choose from and an array of fresh vegetables and salads. The desserts were equally plentiful and lavish. It was a real feast, and as we had eaten far too much, I suggested, when we got up, to take a short walk along the lake. He agreed. But we had hardly taken a few steps, less than a hundred yards or so, when totally unprovoked and unfounded he quite suddenly worked himself up into what can only be described as a defiant, almost hysterical tantrum. I was stunned, and he immediately turned round and stormed off back to the hotel. Only then did it occur to me that doing a simple thing like taking a short walk together was something we had indeed never done before, and it was obviously not an activity to which he took kindly!

But something else happened at this moment. A chord that had yet been untouched broke in me and a growing certainty crept into my consciousness that this incident could not simply be swept aside, that it was the final nail in the coffin of a relationship which had never really been allowed to develop into something deeper and more meaningful.

When in a pensive and thoughtful mood I had finished the walk by myself and returned to our hotel room, he was ready to make amends in his usual way, but I could not listen to his pleas this time. It was as if I had stepped outside of myself and was watching his behaviour like a spectator who was not emotionally involved at all in the scene which took place in front of her.

Two days later, when we made the journey back to London by car, nothing more was said or mentioned about our trip to the Norwegian fjords. I was left to wonder whether anything had impressed him at all.

Chapter Fifteen

When we got back, I began to take positive steps towards a more independent life. I began to take driving lessons and I enrolled at a Teachers' Training College in Acton with the aim of becoming a teacher. I felt mentally stimulated by the lectures and books on English literature, philosophy, psychology and theory of education. The children attended school now from nine in the morning till four in the afternoon, and I could apply myself to my studies. It meant, of course, that I had to study in the evenings, too, once I had settled the children in bed, but I was motivated enough to do so with diligence and dedication. I met up with other women students during college hours, to have a chat or a coffee together.

It felt as if I had finally come to life again.

For the first time, my former personality was returning, as if I was becoming a person in my own right again. And a little observation seemed to highlight the two lives we were living: when I entered our bedroom on one occasion, I could not help noticing that on my bedside table, there was a copy of Jane Austen's 'Mansfield Park,' and on my husband's side was a copy of one of those non-descript, badly constructed stories written in poor taste that you pick up at supermarkets and airports. It appeared to me then as a poignant reminder that common interests and a closeness that came from the heart and mind, and not only from the body were not to be found between us.

Another event took place during this vital time of change in my life, and that was the fact that I started to learn how to drive. I did not find it difficult to sit behind the wheel and follow the instructions given by my instructor. So when my husband suggested that I drive his car, he took me down to Marble Arch and I was expected to take the very busy and complex roundabout there. I was making my way very carefully and somewhat cautiously when he started to shout at me to speed up telling me how disastrous this whole procedure was. I kept my cool and made it home, and though I never drove with him again, I had to admit to myself that I still forgot too often and too easily, perhaps even ignored his complete lack of patience, good-humouredness, self-control and temperance.

In order to get more experience in driving out of the centre of London, I frequently booked a double lesson with my very capable driving instructor. He usually came to pick me up for these longer drives and waited for me downstairs. On one such occasion, I noticed, when I got into the car that he had a book in front of him which I was familiar with. It was a book written by one of G.I. Gurdjieff's pupils. I already possessed a copy of it as it had been sent to me by my friend from college. It seemed such a coincidence that my driving instructor should be reading it.

We had lots to talk about when we were driving along, and he told me that he had arranged to meet a lady who held meetings in her home which could be attended by those who were interested in learning in a more practical way about the ideas of Gurdjieff. He parted that day by saying that he would tell me more about the introductory meeting next time we met.

But it would be sooner than that. Two days later I had my instructor on the phone saying:

'I have here one of my clients who knows the lady in question and offers to accompany you should you want to go and see her. Shall I send him over?'

I answered in the affirmative. And so a meeting was arranged for the following day.

Chapter Sixteen

I was taken to a mews house which was in fact not far from where we lived. I went up the narrow little staircase and entered a room which was partly kitchen and partly living room. The kitchen space to my right, with its shelves openly displaying plates, dishes and mugs, was homely and had a rustic appeal.

Light was coming in from above through a skylight and gave the whole room a warm and welcoming feel. The lady whose name was Rina sat in an armchair. She was crocheting something, and I noticed immediately her very white hair and her kind and friendly face. She gave me an encouraging look saying:

'Come in and sit down.'

At this very moment, I had never been anywhere else: everything that had happened in my life seemed to flow together in the one conviction: I had come home. All my hopes, fears, doubts, struggles, past, present and future, seemed to be put at rest as I was welcomed by her and asked to step in and sit down.

'The kind of mother I have always wished to have,'

Passed through my mind, and years later, when she had indeed become a mother to me, I would be reminded of this moment.

It was as if we had always known each other. I looked at her as she was sitting there, calm, serene, with a smile around her mouth which did not allow me to feel as though I was in front of a stranger, but rather somebody I knew and who knew me. She let her eyes rest on me for a moment and her kind, but discerning look seemed to understand without words the many tears which had never been shed.

I was asked to talk about myself and to say what had brought me there. I answered by telling her that I was married, had lived in Hong Kong, and since my return to England had studied some of the books concerned with Gurdjieff's teaching. She said that if I wished I could come the following Monday when a small group of people, her younger group, would be present, and then I left.

That afternoon and evening I had again that happy feeling which by now indicated to me that another turn had taken place in my life, and I have come to believe that these moments and the incidents that lead up to them are not just sheer coincidence, but are stepping stones being put in our path so that at such crucial times, our journey is not arrested, but advanced swiftly at its most auspicious speed.

The following Monday, I went back in order to attend my first meeting. When she saw me enter, she simply said:

'Oh, you came!'

And indeed, I had to make some excuse at home in order to be there at eight o'clock. But I managed it, and I met the rest of the group that consisted of a young couple, a young lady from Holland who lived in London, and a young man from Australia. I listened while they talked and put their questions to Rina who would answer confidently but quietly after a brief moment of silence.

The group met every Monday evening, and my battle was far from over. I had now the task to explain to my husband what had been happening. I showed him the book, and left it deliberately on the table in case he would want to look at it. But neither then nor later did he give it as much as a glance. I told him that this was something I wanted to pursue and that it involved going out for an hour on Monday nights.

At first he did not seem to mind too much. But he soon began to show open displeasure about the fact that I wanted this hour for myself on a Monday night. Every time I returned, the atmosphere was tense and hostile. In order to show him that these people were very friendly, congenial and well-disposed towards him, I asked him to come along to a small pre-Christmas celebration at Rina's home where together with the older group, we would share a simple meal. He was curious enough to come and sat opposite me at the table. But halfway through the meal, he gave me a disgruntled look making it plain that he did not want to stay in their company any longer. Making our apologies to Rina and the other guests, we had to get up and leave.

That year, on Christmas Eve, I wanted to take the children to the church nearby and I pleaded with him to come along so that we could go as a family. But he declined and was adamant that he wanted to stay behind. His resistance was strong enough to make it difficult for me not to abandon the idea altogether. But I wrapped up the children in warm clothes, put on my own black winter coat and left. When we stepped out of the door, the first snowflakes were falling, and while we were walking along, to the children's delight, more and more snowflakes were coming down.

The church was festively lit and many people had come to celebrate midnight mass. I saw Rina in one of the pews, and I watched the children taking it all in eagerly. It was a wonderful service, and the words spoken by the vicar were meaningful but simply put. When we went home that night, the grumpiness of a displeased husband could not undermine or affect the pleasure I felt about being in touch with something so vital, but which had been denied to me for a very long time.

Chapter Seventeen

When I had passed my driving test, I became the proud owner of a mini, and I immediately began to make full use of this new convenience. When my husband went away on his travels now, I would pack the children into the car on Sundays and we would go and visit places which were of some interest. I showed them around the old university towns of Oxford and Cambridge and the cathedral cities Winchester and Canterbury, all the while providing them with stories and historical data about the cities and their past. We played games while driving and so the time always went by very quickly.

On one occasion, my sister came to stay with us for a while, and here, too, the car came in handy when I wanted to show her places she had not seen before.

But there was also going to be a much bigger event which would unite me with my family and my in-laws as well. My father-in-law celebrated that year his eightieth birthday, and everybody was invited to take part in what was going to be a mammoth celebration. Both my parents and my sister were invited too. It was arranged that we should all board the plane together at Heathrow, and on our arrival in Hong Kong were booked into one of the grand and prestigious hotels alongside the quay.

The celebratory dinner took place in one of the large Chinese restaurants, and as it was customary, an entire floor had been hired for the occasion. All the female members of the family wore the most beautiful Chinese gowns where strands of real gold had been woven into the fabric. They looked stunning. I was allowed to wear an evening gown which I had bought in London. My parents were impressed by the sheer extravagance of it all, and my mother-in-law was suitably impressed by my father's kind and gentle manner.

The dinner itself was a grand affair the style of which was so familiar to me by now. My father-in-law sat between his two wives as his first wife, my mother-in-law, had agreed for the very first time that the second wife should be allowed to be present, too.

Custom demanded that we younger ones all approached his table together during the dinner to bow and raise our glasses to him. When finally everybody got up and said their good-byes, my husband suggested that we have a night cap in the hotel bar. A friend of his joined us. As there was some dancing going on, his friend asked me to have a dance with him. When we sat down again, my husband went on chatting to his friend as before. But when we were in our room, I had to bear the most ferocious attack from him full of jealous venom and wild accusations before he turned over and went to sleep.

The following day, we were all invited to take part in a cruise on board a yacht which belonged to one of my husband's friends. When I sat down next to my father, he asked me:

'And how are things now?'

And I replied shaking my head and remembering last night's ordeal:

'Things don't look good.'

When I glanced at him, he returned my look, and I could see that at that moment he understood. I think we both knew then that it was only a matter of time before something would happen that would turn the tables.

Though the conversation with my father had to remain private and therefore brief, I felt reassured that he knew what was going on and that he responded to my situation with empathy.

Without knowing it, this trip to Hong Kong would turn out to be my last.

Chapter Eighteen

The intensity of my husband's ire and indignation about the fact that I now went out once a week to attend this small group meeting, very quickly became unbearable because of his unbending intolerance. I suddenly experienced something like a rebellion which seemed to come from deep within. Ten years had gone by where I had explored every possible avenue to make it possible for me to live within the confines of this marriage, and yet the smallest of steps that I had taken in order to have something for myself was big enough for him to revert to spiteful rancour and resentfulness. In a flash of liberating self-determination which at the same time released a wave of freeing self-justification, I concluded that enough was enough and that sleeping together as husband and wife had become a lie in the eyes of myself and the children I had given life to. I moved out of the master bedroom and went to sleep in the spare room instead.

But it did not stop there. He now went to the other extreme. He said he was sorry, he said he would change, he said, things would be different. Give him the chance to prove it. Come back to our bedroom. I need you. I want to be with you. We are husband and wife, and I want you as my wife… But I could not, did not want to turn back.

Eventually, the pleading and the knocks on the door became less and less frequent. Then there was silence. I did not even notice that we hardly spoke to each other as we had hardly ever spoken to each other. I continued to go to college, to look after the children, to cook, to take walks through the park, and he went away a lot.

This must have gone on for a good four months when one night he announced that he wanted to talk to me. I thought we might have an argument, at best a discussion. I did not really know exactly what to expect. He sat on the sofa and looked very stern and unforgiving. He did not talk; instead he made three damning statements:

'I don't consider you to be my wife any more. You have been a good mother, but a bad wife. But you are quite a stupid woman as I am going to be very wealthy and rich.'

'I am going to look for a place of my own, and you can stay here for the time being.'

I was dismissed and nothing further was said.

Perhaps I had still hoped for things to turn. It was hard for me to accept the facts which were staring me in the face, but above all I found it difficult to come to terms with his coldness; for feelings had no doubt developed between us in the years which we had shared together – or had they? On close examination, I came to the conclusion that what I felt for him was heartfelt care and concern. Did he not feel the same? I wondered – surely, he must feel something…I had always wanted him to speak to me, to speak his mind, and now, ironically, that he had done so, it turned out to be a rather short and gruesome farewell speech. But I came to accept it – or so I thought – and watched him making plans for his accommodation after he had made up his mind that he was going to move out.

He did not waste any time. He went in search of somewhere suitable to live and found a flat in St. John's Wood. But it had to be furnished first with all the necessary amenities and comfort he was used to before he made his final move. It was agreed that the children could come and visit him at weekends.

I hardly noticed his absence since I was so used to him not being there. But I generally began to feel more relaxed and more comfortable in my own skin; I continued to concentrate on my studies as I was in my final year now, and I even felt freer in the handling of the children as their upbringing had been another matter where we had mostly disagreed.

The group meetings became an integral part of my life. I got to know the people attending them more intimately, and they became my closest friends. On Sundays, 'Sunday activities' were held in the garage down below Rina's flat. During these activities, where I could also bring the children, we gathered together in the morning when the program and an exercise were given. The exercise helped us to work on our inner attention by making a connection between mind and body. At the same time physical activities took place like woodwork, mainly for the men, and for the women sowing, embroidery and other such handicrafts. Some of us were in the kitchen preparing lunch. At the end of the day, we would gather together again and talk about how we had been getting on with the exercise and the various tasks in hand.

It was at the end of such a Sunday spent in the company of my friends when I left there feeling positively energized. I left with the clear notion in my mind that communication has always been the means which enables us to be in contact with our fellowmen. Before I knew what

I was doing, I had taken the direction to my husband's flat in St. John's Wood where the children had been for the day. I had thought that I had given up hope concerning us, but now I discovered that with the help of these people, hope had returned and it gave me the incentive to try and speak to him.

He was not at all glad to see me and reluctantly opened the door to his newly found territory. The children, he told me, were already in bed. I accepted a drink which consisted of three quarters of whisky and a drop of water. I looked around while I was sitting in his living room. The walls were covered all over in cork tiles and a thick carpet concealed the floor which made the room look rather dark. The only furniture apart from two black leather armchairs was a very large piece of music equipment.

I started to talk by mentioning the possibility of a life based on mutual respect and understanding. He immediately interrupted me rudely and decisively. His refusal to listen to what I might have to say was so absolute and dictatorial, his rebuke so total and uncompromising that my mood which had been one of optimism and hopeful endeavour on my arrival began to plunge. Without noticing it, I was hastily gulping down the strong whisky, and while he filled up my glass again, he proclaimed his innocence in this whole affair and washed his hands of anything that might yet occur.

The whisky began to have an effect on me as I was not used to drinking strong spirits. This together with the lethal poison of his words, the denial and rejection on his part, robbed me of every last drop of the positive energy I had felt when I entered, and which had made me come and see him. A bottomless gulf, totally unfathomable in its depth seemed to open up in front of me and a surge of utter hopelessness, despondency and dejection seized hold of me when I realised how futile my undertaking had been. I left feeling that every ounce of goodness, every bit of virtue seemed to be destroyed in me, drowned in whisky and his negativity:

There was no communication, no wisdom, no search for the unknown, no hope, no faith, no love – there was only the dark carpet surrounded by cork tiled walls and the stereo sitting in the corner like a spider watching your every move. There was only despair.

While I sat behind the steering wheel, I felt my foot carelessly pressing down on the accelerator. I went faster and faster, and did not care.

'It will all end as it began,' went through my mind,

As I drove on, until I lost control over the steering wheel. The car began to skid from left to right, turned over and came to a stop on its roof leaning against a tree.

Luckily, there were not many cars on the road. When a car approached, a couple got out and I dimly remember that they helped me to climb out of the window. They called an ambulance and I was taken to the nearest hospital giving name and address of my husband as the next of kin.

He was called and he came to the hospital while I was waiting to be examined. The A&E department was extremely busy that night, and we had to wait for our turn. He quickly told the staff off for being so slow, and I was rushed through a quick examination and told that I could go home. My husband dropped me off and left without saying so much as goodbye.

It seemed truly miraculous that I came out of this accident unscathed. The next day, I discovered a large bruise on my left leg and a big bump on my forehead. Apart from that, I seemed unharmed. When I went to see Rina, she asked me what had happened, and I told her the whole incident about my visit and what had followed, and the way I felt just before the accident. She listened, but said nothing.

It was only after two weeks or so had passed that I began to behave in a somewhat strange manner: I would walk aimlessly for long distances, and when I began to feel hot, I would strip off my socks and just throw them away. A ring on my finger which I suddenly thought did not suit me anymore was likewise thrown away. I walked all the way to Rina's flat, and she asked me to sit down.

'You are in shock,' she said to me.

'No,' I said, 'I feel alright'.

But I was anything but alright. I began to stop people in the street and would ask them odd questions like:

'Where is the ladder to be found that leads to heaven?'

On one occasion, I walked all the way to Paddington Station, and as I had no money on me, I stopped passers-by and begged them for money so that I could buy myself a cup of tea. This odd behaviour remained unchecked until one day, I followed Rina who I knew attended a poetry class in the City Lit, an adult learning centre in London, on a certain day and knocked on the door.

For her this was the signal that something had to be done. She took my hand, called a taxi and drove off with me.

'But I am alright, Rina, really I am,' I said with conviction; for, indeed, in her presence I felt that nothing could harm me anymore. From her determined look, however, I could make out that we were not exactly going home.

From that moment on, Rina assumed full responsibility for me which involved looking after me and making sure that I received any kind of treatment which might turn out to be necessary.

Chapter Nineteen

Rina stayed with me while we were waiting in the hospital. I felt quite anxious by then, and in order to reassure myself, I put my hand on hers and she let it be. After the examination which was conducted by one of their doctors, it was decided that I should be sent to a mental hospital in South London.

I was shown to a large ward where I was given a bed and bedside table. There were a lot of patients sitting around in the community hall all of whom, I became dimly aware, seemed drugged and lifeless, and though I, too, was soon administered some kind of medication, I remained more alert than the people sitting listlessly around me.

I don't know what would have happened to me had I stayed there for any length of time; but after three days I was fetched and taken back to Rina. She took the decision that I should be taken to a clinic in Harrow-on-the-Hill where she knew one of the leading psychiatrists there.

Rina seemed to have endless patience with me. Being without medication after leaving the hospital, I had lost all sense of reality. All the barriers which normally keep us in check had fallen away, and I talked and chatted, and chatted and talked ceaselessly while she kept her attention quietly focused on me all the time. In her presence, I became like a little child again who knew that her mother's care would protect it, and who, not having learnt yet the limitations and restrictions of the adult world, is allowed to communicate everything that went through its mind. And still, I kept on babbling until I tired and gave everybody a well-earned rest from listening to me.

Again, we had to wait, this time in a waiting-room furnished with comfortable armchairs, and again, I began to feel quite uncertain about what would happen to me. This time, in order to reassure myself, I made the sudden, but firm declaration:

'When I see this doctor, I shall only speak French!'

Rina went into the consulting room first, and the door was shut behind her. I sat down on the nearby staircase: I did not only behave like a child, I also felt the dependency of a child. I quickly had become used to the idea that Rina was always there for me, and in that sense, she undoubtedly had committed herself to looking after me like a mother. It seemed that, for the first time in my adult life, I was allowed to experience what it is like to have someone by your side who you could trust implicitly and who you could rely on no matter what the circumstances.

I finally was called in and saw a man with very bushy eyebrows above his spectacles looking at me with keen interest. In front of him sat Rina on a chair. The moment I entered, I sat down on another chair and immediately started to speak effortlessly in French. This went on for a while as no one interrupted me, and I went on telling them the story of my life. Both Rina and the doctor understood, as he told me later, perfectly well what I was saying.

When I finally stopped, I looked at him again. He was still silently watching me, and suddenly wanting to provoke him, I made one big sweeping movement with my right hand and cleaned his desk of everything which had been on it, picture frames, ornaments and all. I caught Rina's face who seemed to look at him imploringly. I, too, looked at him again, this time quite fearlessly, and assessed his face while he continued to watch quietly, from below his bushy eyebrows, every move of mine. He did not express any surprise or alarm. His look was steady and reassuring, and at that moment, I submitted to his unwavering steadfastness. He, on the other hand, accepted me there and then as a patient because, as he told me much later, my case had roused his interest and presented a challenge to him in his capacity as a doctor.

I only vaguely realised then that he had not only listened to my story, but that he had done so with care, all the while studying my mental state with a professional eye. It was to be the beginning of a lifelong friendship based on mutual trust. Looking at each other then, in his consulting room, was like a moment of truth.

I prattled on regardless while we were taken to my room, and another doctor arrived in order to administer my first medication which was meant to calm me down. With the instinctive suspicion of the mentally ill, I refused to take it and gave him a proper sermon instead about what he should or should not do. This went on for another half hour, until I heard Rina quietly say:

'Just consider how tired I must feel after all this!' and at these words, I burst into tears and willingly swallowed my first tablets. I lay down on my bed and soon enough, I became calmer and eventually went to sleep. A very eventful day, very exhausting for those around me, had finally come to an end.

Meanwhile, my husband was informed and he was asked to come forward and pay for my stay in the clinic. All this went on without my knowing anything about it. As for me, I felt safe and carefree in my new environment and soon made friends with the girl who occupied the room opposite and who told me she was being treated for drug addiction. I still continued to be mainly controlled by my impulses, and so, one day when I found out that there was a hairdresser on the ground floor, I quickly decided to change my blond hair to a bright titian red which Rina commented on when she came to see me by saying:

'You do look funny with your red hair!'

I felt almost happy during these days as I felt cared for and looked after. Towards the end of my stay there, when my father and sister came to see me, I was allowed out for a weekend, and I promptly took them over to Rina's garage to show them what it was used for. Unfortunately, she was away that weekend and therefore never met my father and sister.

As my sister told me later, my father suggested that I should come home and be looked after there, but I refused and told him that I wanted to stay where I was. My father left feeling greatly upset about my condition even though I had already greatly improved.

My stay in the clinic was nearly over. After six weeks I was allowed to return home, but I was told that I must continue the treatment by visiting my doctor in his consulting rooms in Devonshire Place which I promised to do.

Chapter Twenty

At first all went well. I continued to see my doctor regularly; he had started a new treatment of injections which was meant to keep me on an even keel. My condition improved, and, as it turned out, I was soon confronted with new circumstances in my life where I needed to be strong and needed to cope.

First of all, I had to move out of the flat where I was still living as the lease had run out and could not be renewed. My husband told me that I could go ahead and look for a house. One of my friends from Rina's older group was into property, and when I asked him whether he could assist me, he was only too willing to do so. With his help, I soon found a suitable property in a tree-lined avenue of West London. It had a front and a back garden and the house was spacious and well-proportioned inside. It had four bedrooms on the first floor, and downstairs there was a combined open living and dining room; adjacent was a large conservatory. The kitchen was large and well-equipped. I was soon able to move in having found some second-hand furniture in an antiques' market. The children who had been looked after partly by my husband and partly by Rina, especially my daughter, came back to me, and life seemed almost to take on a normal course again.

But this respite was short-lived and did not last long as meanwhile, my husband had met a young Austrian girl, and as she, too, had become pregnant, he wanted to get married as soon as possible. He needed a divorce quickly and therefore tried to put it through swiftly, yet forcefully by pleading for full custody of the children as it was his intention to send both children to boarding schools. My doctor put me in touch with a solicitor who specialised in divorces, and the terrifying prospect of divorce proceedings began. I dreaded the day when I was meant to appear in court and face my husband who, I knew, would do everything in his power to have his way.

The fateful day arrived, and I got ready. Luckily, someone from the older group who had been asked to keep an eye on me offered to accompany me to my day of Calvary. In the courtroom I was asked to take the witness stand, and I had time to glance at my husband who was seated in one of the benches wearing an elegant light grey suit. His solicitor and barrister were seated on either side of him whereas I had come on my own. With a trace of sadness I looked at him while he avoided looking at me, and the words passed through my mind:

'I have been married to you for more than ten years, and now you want to fight me over the children.'

But I was soon under attack from both his solicitor and his barrister and had even to answer questions about my interest in a certain 'cult'. It took all my attention, composure and sangfroid to respond adequately to the many questions which were fired at me in quick succession. I was fighting for my children, and my mother's instinct kept me going until I finally heard the judge's voice:

'I see nothing wrong with this woman, and it shall therefore be shared custody,' and the hammer came down.

When I stepped down, I thought for a moment that my knees would give way, but I managed to leave the room, my head held up high and meet my friend who had been waiting outside the door. Then the whole ordeal caught up with me, and tears where running down my cheeks, silently and abundantly, while we were driving back to my house. It was all over.

The experience had shaken me through and through; but I recovered, and I had to turn my attention now to yet another pressing matter: I knew that my son being ten and a half years old had reached an age when his father would insist that he was sent to a good boarding school. I wanted to choose the school myself and asked Rina for advice. She was able to recommend me a school which she spoke highly of as two boys from among the many people she knew had been happy there. I fully agreed with her that in order to perform well in school, children must be allowed to feel at ease with their environment, and I therefore went to visit the school with my son. The teacher we spoke to was most friendly and accommodating which gave me the impression that my son would be in good hands there. He asked him to sit a test right there and then as the time for admission was fast running out. He was a bright boy, and the test presented no obstacle to him: he was accepted into the school, and when we left I felt confident that I had made a good choice for him.

When I finally took him there and we had to say goodbye to each other, it was a heart-breaking moment for both of us. But the matron who was in charge of looking after the boys was very reassuring, and I left him in the hope that he would soon settle down in his new school. During the first few months, however, I made sure that he was alright by visiting him regularly on Sunday afternoons.

When all was dealt with and organised, I received the sad news that my father was in hospital and had undergone an operation. Then I was told that a second one was necessary. He did not survive this second operation and passed away while staying in hospital.

I had always felt close to my father, and this news came therefore as a terrible shock to me. I made preparations to go and attend his funeral which was going to be a cremation, and I took my son with me who had loved his grandfather.

When we were all assembled in the hall which the crematorium provided for this purpose, the small orchestra in the background began to play my father's favourite violin concerto by Brahms. The music which was so familiar to me pierced through my heart and I began to sob uncontrollably. My whole body was shaking as I tried to get a hold of myself. My sister who was sitting to my left did not move at all: no kind or consoling gesture was made, no indication given that she was sharing the loss I was feeling at that moment: there was no acknowledgement at all of my strong emotion the signs of which were so obvious – I stood alone in my grief when suddenly I felt the small hand of my son on my lap, and this was enough to restore my inner balance and to be ready for the aftermath of the funeral.

My mother had prepared a simple meal at home and had invited two of their closest friends. Sadly, my father's death did not bring us closer together in any way, for by the time we arrived at home, as always, I had to hide what I was feeling; it even appeared that by then, when the actual funeral was behind us, they were almost out of place – my mother and sister seemed to cope so much better and had everything so much more under control – no one was there with whom I could have shared or talked about what I had just experienced.

'He was a good man,' was the comment which was made.

It seemed to me that nothing that was said during the meal came from the heart to which I could have responded. As always, it all remained in the domain of the good and proper. But I was glad to have had the opportunity to say farewell to my beloved father, and I was equally glad that I had shared this moment with my son.

Chapter Twenty-One

As he had predicted, my now ex-husband was able to lead a very affluent lifestyle when he got married a second time. He lived in a mansion in St. John's Wood; in the double garage stood his lifelong ambition, a Rolls Royce and a Porsche, and a driver and housemaid were accommodated in the basement. The children visited him frequently at weekends as there was now a new baby in the family and a second one on the way.

My son usually came to me on a Saturday, whenever he was allowed out, and very often I had to listen to his grievances and dry his tears before I would let him set off on his own to go and stay with his father and his new family as this was where he wanted to be.

My daughter who was still living with me was also looking forward to her weekends in St. John's Wood, and one day she returned to me and said:

'Daddy says, I can have the entire third floor to myself if I come to stay with him.'

As I had always adopted the attitude that the children should feel free to choose where they wanted to be in order to spare them the heartache of two parents arguing over them, I had to let her go, too, knowing that the distress and agony which this step would cause me would have to be borne by myself alone.

Until then, my mental health was, though fragile, fairly stable as I continued my visits to my doctor on a regular basis. When he had given me the news that my ex-husband had come to see him and that, rather than enquiring about my state of health, he had simply told him that he did not wish to pay any more bills, he was kind enough to offer me an arrangement where I paid him a minimum amount of money for each visit.

I had now to face the fact that both children preferred to stay with their father and his new family, in an environment that was both luxurious and grand in every way. Without having been consulted, I was given the news that a boarding school had been found for my daughter, and that she was only too keen to go. She was by then sixteen years old. It seemed as if my every right as a mother had slipped through my fingers, and I did not have the strength to do anything about it. I felt abandoned, rejected, and my heart was craving for a sign of affection from either of the children. But I hardly saw them anymore.

At the same time, money was running out. There were repairs to the house which needed to be paid and which consumed the savings I had. Inflation was such that the little money I received as maintenance was not adequate any longer even to support just myself. At this crucial point when I would have needed his support, I stopped seeing my doctor.

I began to get up every morning in a cold, unheated and empty house, and before I knew it, I would be in floods of tears. Not understanding what was happening to me and never having heard of a mental illness called depression, I soldiered on regardless. Soon I did not see anybody anymore. Not only did I stop seeing my doctor, but I stayed away from Rina and her groups as well. Totally withdrawn from normal life and penniless, I did not know anymore where to turn. The only person I spoke to in those days was my kind neighbour who would chat to me over the garden fence and who could probably hear me sob inside the empty house. Her warm-hearted words were always able to comfort me for a little while.

I tried to read, but could not focus on more than one sentence; I tried to feed myself, but could hardly get anything down. I grew numb, without any feeling or emotion, and yet the tears never stopped.

'What is wrong with me,' I asked helplessly, without being able to find an answer.

It was during those dark days that I received a call from my mother telling me that she had been admitted to hospital again because of another heart attack. She had been in hospital before, and I knew that she had a heart condition, but this time when I heard the news, without understanding why, I burst into tears as if I was saying goodbye. And yet, she said in quite a motherly way:

'Don't cry. I will come home again,' and she did come home, and was looking forward to celebrating her seventieth birthday the same month.

I had promised to be there. But when I tried repeatedly and in desperation to pack my case, I did not manage it. In my confused state, I could not get organised, get myself together and leave – I would have needed a helping hand to make sure I was ready for the trip.

Her birthday came and the telephone rang all day. Not knowing why, I could not bring myself to pick it up. When at long last, it rang once more at ten o'clock at night, I finally held the receiver in my hand and I heard my ex-husband say:

'We tried to reach you all day. Your mother died of a heart attack this morning.'

When I thought things could not get any worse, I had yet to dig deeper in order to keep my head above water. I was unable to attend my mother's funeral just as I was unable to assist my sister in the clearance of the parental home. Only much later could I put the feelings of guilt to rest by understanding that I was then in the grip of a severe and acute depression and that, in a strange way, I had said goodbye to my mother over the phone when she had rung me.

Weeks went by during which my only release from emotional turmoil and tension were the tunes of the Shakespearian songs I taught myself to play on my old school recorder. Every morning, I would diligently practise until I became quite good at playing them. It sounded nice to my ears and it gave me a focus of some kind.

One day, I received a call from my sister to tell me that she had got engaged, and she invited me to come and stay for a while. I jumped at the opportunity, and this time, under the duress of a lot of emotional uncertainty, I made sure that I was really going.

As her flat was opposite our parental home, I thought it would give me the chance to say goodbye to it in my own quiet way. But a day after my arrival, her fiancé joined us unexpectedly, and I was told in no uncertain terms that I could no longer stay as her flat was small, too small for the three of us.

'If you stay, we will have our first argument because of you, and I don't want that,' she said to her defence.

It had cost me a great effort to come and see her, and I was, without being fully aware of it, not well enough to make any clear decisions; realising that, my sister simply rang my aunt and told her that she was sending me over to her home.

Hurt and bruised, I left in order to visit first my aunt and then an old friend of mine. While the two of us were sitting together in a pub, he watched me staring blankly at the menu and he asked gently:

'When was the last time you saw your doctor?'

In surprise, I answered:

'Why?'

'I think you ought to go and see him.'

'Well, I manage, don't I?' I replied.

'Do go and see him,' he insisted and left it at that.

Back in the isolation of my house, I had time to think about his remark, and after some considerable time of wavering hesitation, I picked up the phone and gave his secretary a call. An appointment was made.

Chapter Twenty-Two

When I first sat in one of those comfortable large armchairs again facing my doctor, I felt a great sense of relief. We talked, and I experienced afresh the sensation which seemed to come from being near him and which spoke of care, concern, and even love.

Having the vision of a great doctor, he knew when to speak with authority, when to listen sympathetically, when to say nothing at all or when to say something with much emphasis. At times he would just chat in a nonchalant manner to make you feel relaxed and at ease. Underlying it all was a close bond which meanwhile had developed between us and which allowed me to see a fatherly figure in him who cared enough to take a real interest in my wellbeing and to whom I could therefore entrust my problems, health-related or otherwise.

When I saw him a second time, he took great care to explain to me that just talking was not enough and that he had to start treating me again by prescribing some medication, but that it was for depression this time. I accepted his statement without any further questioning, and for the first time I could give a name to my condition.

I somehow felt very strongly that, by visiting him again, I had turned the corner and that from now on things could only get better.

He enquired about Rina and when I told him that I had not seen her all this time, he encouraged me to look her up.

And so, after the consultation had ended, I walked over to her flat for the first time in many months. She greeted me as if she had only seen me yesterday, no questions asked, just:

'Come and sit down and pour yourself a drink.'

And when I sat down facing her, I felt for the second time that I had come home; at that moment, I regained a kind of inner balance which had been shaken so dramatically since I had last seen her. The numbness I had experienced for what had seemed to me an eternity, gave way to a feeling of happiness and joyfulness. She gave me a cheerful smile while, as always, letting her eyes rest on me.

I told her that I had just said goodbye to my doctor, and immediately she said:

'Oh, good! How is the old man?'

It was as if I had never been away.

As I was not ready to return to her group, I began to drop in on her on a regular basis. She gave me a set of her house keys and said that I could come as often as I liked. Very often, I would drop by in the early evening hours so as to meet some of the group members before the group meeting started, and I would withdraw to the spare room while the meeting was going on. It was encouraging to see everyone again, and quite frequently I would stay on after the meeting, when everyone had left. There was a second bedroom in her flat, and when it got too late to go home, she suggested that I stay for the night. I would then leave the following morning. This happened quite frequently, and soon I kept an overnight bag in that second bedroom and decorated it to my liking. In return for her kindness, I began to do little chores for her around the house. These included going shopping, arranging flowers or serving tea when someone came to visit her.

In later years I was always there to look after her in every possible way I could or as far as she would allow me to do so.

I especially enjoyed spending the evenings with her. In winter it meant that we sat opposite each other next to the gas-fire while the two cats were asleep on the cushion in front of it. These evenings were filled with a sense of peaceful and tranquil serenity which had a healing quality about it making me feel as though I was sheltered from the outside world and allowing conversation to flow from the trivial to the more profound. I always learnt something from these conversations with her, something which I could take away with me.

She was in the habit of crocheting a bedcover or a waistcoat for herself or for somebody else. I still wear the two waistcoats she made for me with pride. While she was thus working away, I could see that at the same time, she was practising keeping her attention on the work in hand as well as on her vis-à-vis. For entertainment, we quite often played a word game similar to Scrabble.

The more I saw of her, the deeper the affection grew between us, thus becoming a very close bond indeed.

As she also had to look after a group in Yorkshire, she spent every other weekend in the north. An old barn building had been acquired and transformed into a habitable house which could accommodate up to forty people. It was situated outside of Settle and could only be reached by a small uneven track. After the last bend, the house finally appeared, seemingly out of nowhere to welcome the arriving guests with its smoking chimneys and brightly lit windows. Behind the white wooden gate, there was a garden surrounding the house, and as it stood on an exposed piece of land, it offered a wonderful open view over the countryside. There was no other habitation in sight, and the only creatures to be seen were the grazing sheep.

Both the London and the Northern groups came together here on special occasions. This meant that at Easter the big hall was richly decorated, a festive meal would be prepared in the kitchen, and in order to seat everyone, the four long tables would be arranged in the shape of a square. The Easter Vigil was celebrated in a village church nearby. When we returned, the Easter eggs were painted so that they would be ready for the children the following morning.

At Whitsun or Pentecost, the theme given usually centred round communication and was studied in various ways. But there was also the 'party of pleasure' which usually consisted of an outing of some kind or a picnic.

And there was the summer week. People were divided up in small teams, and every team was responsible for a certain task around the house like housework, gardening, cooking, serving or washing-up as the case may be. There was always a theme given for the week which included study as well as inner work in the form of special exercises which kept us focused both on ourselves and our neighbour. There was plenty of opportunity for self-observation and self-study which helped us to get in touch with a deeper and more authentic sense of self. And there were the movements we were encouraged to practise in the movement class, some of which increased our inner attention, others simply awakened in us a yearning for the divine as it can be present inside all of us. These movements were accompanied by music on the piano.

As I was not allowed yet to participate fully in all the activities, I usually accompanied Rina on the train and I was what she called a 'guest' which meant I was only there to watch and learn and to be among them, while remaining in close proximity to Rina herself.

These memorable occasions were part of an education which would stay with us and shape our lives in a new, but definite way. They created in me a sounder understanding of the profundity of inner work, and they taught me a deep reverence for everything sacred.

With the combined effort of both Rina and my doctor, my battered and bruised outer shell, too, could begin to recover. Gradually, I grew more self-confident and outgoing. But she also saw to it that I was made aware of the rough edges in my character of which there were plenty and which required work.

As Rina allowed me to invite my doctor for a simple lunch from time to time, it gave me great pleasure to see these two people who had taken on such a vital role in my life, sitting and conversing together in my presence.

Chapter Twenty-Three

I soon had to turn my attention to yet another urgent matter. There was the house which had become too big for me and which I could not maintain any longer as money had run out.

When there was major repair necessary on the roof, I gave my ex-husband a call and begged him to help me pay for it. Reluctantly and only after he had voiced at great length his displeasure about my request he agreed, but also said:

'Sell the house.'

I knew he was right and that this was good practical advice. I therefore began to visit certain districts and areas which I preferred as a location, and when I had made a list of streets which I particularly liked, I started to consult estate agents in those localities. The search had been on for six months when, to my delight, a flat which I could afford was put up for sale in my favourite street.

It was a one-bedroom flat on the second floor overlooking beautiful private gardens to which I would have access. The flat itself was small, but compact and very much to my liking. The view was its most striking aspect. I knew that I was able to purchase the flat from the sale of the house, and still have money left over which could be put away and kept as my savings.

A friendly neighbour put me in touch with a lady who expressed interest in buying the house. She came to inspect it and immediately fell in love with it. It all happened so quickly, and everything was sorted out so smoothly and in such a short space of time that it could not have been easier. It was as if I had been given a helping hand in it all.

I sold the furniture which I had bought for the house as it was too big and bulky in the small flat, and acquired a few items of simple modern design to furnish living room, dining area and bedroom. When I finally was given the key and moved in, I felt happy and relieved to leave behind a house which in itself was lovely and beautiful, but where I had experienced a lot of grief and unhappiness, and where I no longer felt secure. Now I could have my windows wide open, breathe in the fresh air coming from the old trees in the garden, and feel safe. I kept a sofa bed in the living room in case one of the children would want to visit me and stay for the night.

For the first time I felt free in body and spirit. Those shackles which had not allowed me to enjoy life and to live it to the full, began to be loosened one by one. I experienced the pleasant sensation of being able to make my own decisions, to trust my own mind and simply to be who I was. This made me appreciate my new environment in a uniquely fresh and imaginative way. I cherished this sense of transformation which this gave me and which grew stronger day by day. I began to explore my new area, and as I got to know my neighbours, both next door and in the street, I soon became a happy and esteemed member of the surrounding community.

In summer I began to make full use of the beautiful gardens. I often took a book together with a little canvas folding chair which Rina had given me to spend the afternoon there, and when a friend came to see me, it would be tea and biscuits in the garden on a fine day. I also began to turn my attention to writing poetry again – something I had sorely missed. I had always had a disposition for writing, and so I began to put pen to paper again to express my thoughts and feelings. When I read some of them to Rina for whom poetry was a very familiar subject, she encouraged me to continue with it.

Chapter Twenty-Four

It was late summer 1982. I still saw little of the children who had left school by now and had moved on to university. On one occasion, my daughter came and made use of the sofa-bed, but left again the following morning; and so, at long last, with my recovery well on its way, I had the clear-sightedness, presence of mind and mental stability to conclude:

'You have been given the opportunity to do something for yourself now,'

And remembering that I had always wanted to study German literature, I yielded to a sudden impulse and made my way to Senate House which is part of the University of London and where enquiries could be made regarding an application for one of the many different colleges.

'Is it too late to apply?'

I asked the man behind the desk in the entrance hall.

'Well, I'm afraid so, Madam, but let me check,' he answered. He was going through his list when I heard him say:

'You are in luck! Bedford College in Regent's Park is still interviewing for places.'

I was delighted and went home to make arrangements for my application.

When all was sent off, I did not have to wait long. I received a letter in which I was asked to come for an interview.

As I made my way to Regent's Park, I wondered what would be expected of me. I needn't have worried. I was introduced to a very nice man, one of the professors at the department, who asked me to sit down in his office.

We talked about the books I had read and discussed the reason why I had chosen to study German literature. I was then given a poem and was allowed some time to read it and to reflect on it before he asked me for my opinion, what the poem was saying to me, and how I would elucidate what the poet had been trying to express in this poem.

With his help, I was able to analyse the poem quite successfully, and when I left I had the distinct feeling that I had done enough to be accepted.

Two weeks later, I was holding a letter in my hand which stated that I was now a student of Bedford College and gave details about a meeting to welcome new students and to familiarise them with the facilities of the college.

This introduction was the beginning of a time for me which I will never forget. I attended and enjoyed the many lectures as they were presented to us. I learned to listen and take notes. The reading list we were given was long, but I enjoyed plunging into book after book, learning all about their authors and analysing their content which was then put into their historical context.

We also learnt about the origin of the Germanic languages: we discussed Old German texts and the beautiful rich medieval literature which was particularly satisfying and inspiring to me.

French was my second choice, and I profited here from the fact that I had already a good grounding in the language. It was a two year course at the end of which there would be a written and oral examination.

I had the bright idea, before sitting the exam, to write to my former French family who, meanwhile, had moved to a small village outside Nice, and I asked Madame whether she would allow me to come and stay for two weeks in order to brush up my French. She wrote back in the affirmative. I was soon on my way and spent two pleasant weeks at their large house with its swimming pool outside and lines of olive trees growing behind the house.

I made new friends. I was not the only mature student among the first year students and I got to know some of the others when we had lunch in the canteen. I also mixed with some of the younger students. We got on well together and always had plenty to talk about.

When one of my friends told me that she intended to join the choir of Imperial College where you did not have to go through an audition, she persuaded me to come along. And I was glad that I did. For I discovered that I greatly enjoyed the rehearsals which were once a week in the early evening hours and always were in preparation of a concert given at a later stage. We were asked to sell as many tickets as we could manage to both family and friends.

It was a wonderful experience for me to sing through an entire concert with the voices divided up into sopranos, altos, tenors and bass, and the solo artists performing their arias intermittently, while the orchestra provided the background music. In time, I thus came to know the many requiems and masses written by the old masters, but sometimes we would also sing the music of a modern composer.

Rina came to nearly every concert that was given. It was nice to know that there was a familiar face among the audience who had especially come to hear you sing. On one occasion, it was my daughter who had bought a ticket and we could see each other and chat during the interval.

While I was walking in front of her, I suddenly heard her call from behind:

'Margaret!'

I turned round and realised that, indeed, it was her who was calling me.

'Why do you call me Margaret?' I asked perplexed, and her reply was:

'I thought, you might not want to let the others know that you have a grown-up daughter.'

Well, she was by then eighteen years old!

Here again, I had made friends with some of the participants, and though most of the time the age difference between us did not seem to matter much as we all shared a common interest, it could happen that I became uncomfortably aware of the fact that I was older than the majority of them – but as I was blessed with a good complexion which made me look and feel young, I fitted in quite easily.

It was the age of Margaret Thatcher, and in the second year, we were told that Bedford College was going to be amalgamated with Royal Holloway College out in Egham near Windsor. The merger would take place the following year, when we were in our third year which would be spent at a university of our choice in Germany.

I made good use of my time in Germany. I had chosen Saarbruecken University as my destination and was looking forward to savouring aspects of student life there. I found myself a nice room with a view over the town; it was rented out by two old ladies who were sisters and lived together in the same house. While attending the lectures which I had signed up for, I noticed to my amusement that many of the female students were in the habit of doing their knitting when listening to the lecturer.

But I kept the attendance of lectures to a minimum and spent the rest of the time reading widely by taking books out of the university library. All the authors for whom there had been little time during the term, were now on my reading list, and so I spent a good deal of time in my room becoming acquainted with more and more of literature's great advocates, some better known than others.

When we returned, it was time to make arrangements for the continuation of our studies at what had now become 'Royal Holloway and Bedford New College,' RHBNC for short. As the new college was quite a distance away from London, I decided to go and live on campus. A coach was conveniently at our disposal should we want to go to Central London. We would get off the coach just in front of the back entrance to the British Museum.

I made use of this convenience as often as I could to visit Rina and occasionally my doctor who I still saw from time to time. I was always glad to see them and every time there was news to bring and stories to tell.

Royal Holloway was surrounded by beautiful woods where you could take a stroll when you wanted to have a break from all the mental exertion. In spring, there were the many rhododendron bushes adding splashes of vivid colour to the otherwise green environment. And, of course, there was Windsor so nearby that one only had to walk across some woodland and fields to arrive at the park's enclosure.

There were tennis courts for a game of tennis and a busy tuck shop where you could buy the all-important 'Royal Holloway' sweat shirt or a Royal Holloway mug as a souvenir.

I was able to be part of the choir of the college that met regularly in the picture gallery for rehearsals, and apart from giving a concert at intervals, we would also sing in the chapel on a Sunday morning.

We had soon formed a small group of friends who met regularly, mainly at mealtimes in the dining hall. Two of them were mature students like myself and the two younger ones were studying psychology and English literature. In the evenings, we often got together in the common room to watch 'Spitting Image,' a politically infused TV program where the politicians were presented by caricatured puppets, and from this program, we had adopted the humorous expression: 'You either shut up or you will have your head chopped off,' when we were in disagreement and wanted to tease one another.

It was a great delight to me to be part of an old English tradition which has survived up to this day and continues to form and shape the lives of educated young men and women. I had the privilege to be one among them and fulfil my dream of having at long last the academic education I had always craved for.

During all this time, I had not seen the children at all and I had got used to the idea that they preferred to live their own lives which included being with their father. But one day, when I was queuing in the dining hall, I suddenly spotted the two faces of my son and daughter at the entrance. After the first moments of embarrassment and surprise had passed, I invited them to come to my room. My son immediately went off to explore the college by himself, but my daughter followed me in order to inspect my students' quarters. As soon as we were alone in my room, she was quick to criticize me, and I could see that the notion of her mother being a student like herself and even living on campus disconcerted her; it conflicted with the image she had of me as somebody who used to tuck her in at night:

'And it will be blue jeans and discos next!' she exclaimed, and her protest was obvious.

I reassured her that I had come here to study and not to amuse myself, and after some further explanations, she began to realise that perhaps the whole idea was not quite as absurd as she had first imagined.

My son, on the contrary, was quite happy to accept that his mother had decided to become what he called a 'super-duper doctor'.

During the fourth and final year of my studies, when I began to work towards the final exams, I practised above all how to present my argument in the form of an essay within the time limit of sixty minutes. There was a list of topics we could choose from, and in my room, I would argue my case again and again until I became more skilled at it.

When I was finally seated in the exam room, I had no difficulty in writing down what I wanted to say, and yet still finish in time.

With the exams being behind us, the sun came out at last, as it had been raining steadily; the time of labour was over and the wait for the results could begin. I received an upper second.

Both Rina and my doctor were delighted with this result, and Rina and I celebrated the end of my course with a slap-up meal in her favourite French restaurant which was just around the corner from where she lived.

To make job hunting more efficient, my doctor had suggested having business cards printed where I could now add BA (hons).

But as it should turn out, a job was just around the corner. When I was walking up to Notting Hill Gate which was part of my wider neighbourhood, a sign came to my notice which I must have passed many times and had never looked at. It said:

'Astron School of Languages. English and Foreign Languages.'

I walked up the stairs there and then. A man was sitting behind the reception desk who introduced himself as the manager of the school.

I said with absolute confidence:

'I have a degree in German literature and I am a trained teacher – do you perhaps need a teacher for German?'

He looked at me and after a few words were exchanged, he added:

'We might need someone to teach on a one-to-one basis as well as in class. I will let you know.'

A first step had been taken.

Chapter Twenty-Five

Two weeks later I received a call from him and he asked me to come for an interview. When I arrived, he took me to a classroom and said to me:

'Imagine I don't speak any German at all,' and he added looking quite smug:

'Actually I do; I lived in Munich for a while. But think of this as being the very first lesson – how would you proceed?'

I was slightly taken aback; I had to ask for time, and so I said questioningly:

'Without a book?' He must have understood and therefore added:

'Just a minute,' and left the room.

I took the opportunity to let a plan arise in my head, and when he returned, I was ready.

The rest was easy, and he concluded:

'You can start next week.'

I quickly felt at home in the environment of the school. The manager was a very congenial kind of a man, and the rest of the staff was equally easy to get on with. The atmosphere in the school was very relaxed, and I fitted in perfectly.

I worked on a freelance basis, and there was a constant demand for private tuition on a one-to-one basis, but twice a week I also had a class of seven to ten students wanting to make a start in learning the language.

The teaching was so varied, and the people who wanted to learn German came from such diverse backgrounds that there was never a dull moment. They came from all walks of life: there were the Japanese air stewardesses who wanted to add German to their repertoire of languages, there were my four young students from South Africa who found it quite easy to pick up and speak the language, there were business men aspiring to become executives when they would be asked to go to Germany – the range was endless, and I even helped an A-level student to write her German essays.

I never failed to plan my lessons, as this was the simple secret to good teaching. Very soon, I came to realise that I much preferred to teach adults rather than children, and began to enjoy my work very much. I always succeeded in establishing a special relationship with my private students and tailored my lessons to their individual needs; gaining experience and confidence and continuing to improve my style of teaching, I knew that I had found the kind of work that suited me down to the ground.

At the same time, I began to consider taking up my studies again and applying for a master's degree course. I discussed this possibility with one of my former tutors, and as he encouraged me to go ahead with it, I did not hesitate any longer and handed in my application.

I opted for a two year part-time course so that I could continue to work at the same time. All the seminars took place at the Institute for Germanic Studies and were held in the evenings. The subject was German literature of the 20th century, and professors from different colleges came to teach us. We were only seven to ten students in all and so could enjoy a close supervision by our tutors.

Because of the nature of the course, we were now able to focus on fewer authors and study them in greater depth. There were the two giants of the 20th century, Thomas Mann and Hermann Hesse, but there was also Nietzsche's philosophy which had formed and shaped the thinking of the 20th century German authors. We also had to study poetry which meant becoming acquainted with the outstanding poetry of Rainer Maria Rilke.

The exquisite language and the form of his sonnets impressed me very much, and because I was interested in poetry, I began to emulate him and practised writing poems in sonnet form until I eventually found my own way of expression.

My dissertation was to be on Hermann Hesse. By studying his major and minor works, as well as his poetry, I came to understand him as a man and writer who continued to search for the truth, and his journey through life found expression in all his novels; never tiring of leading the reader along the path where questions were asked rather than answers given, he succeeded in writing some extraordinary and thought-provoking books.

It was a substantial piece of work I had to write, and I struggled with the length of it, but I enjoyed the fact that it allowed me to become thoroughly acquainted with one particular author whom I was interested in, and to arrive at my own conclusions in the course of my research.

When the dissertations were handed in, we prepared ourselves for the oral examination held by an external examiner. Questions about the dissertation would also be asked and discussed.

It was a nerve-racking experience. When I was told that I had passed, but that I had to rewrite certain sections of my dissertation, nobody was more indignant than Rina who had kept a close eye on my progress.

Meanwhile, I continued to teach and never seemed to tire of starting afresh with a new group or a private student which helped me to keep my lessons interesting and stimulating.

Rina had by now reached an age when she needed a bit more looking after, and I was glad that I could repay her somewhat for what I had received and was still receiving. Of course, there were also the members of the group who would often prepare a meal for her or bring her a special treat. Though she had become less mobile, she still travelled up north every other weekend, and I helped her pack her suitcase and accompanied her to King's Cross from where she would take the train. While she was away, I looked after her two Siamese cats, often did a bit of cleaning if the cleaning lady had failed to show up and put fresh flowers in her sitting room, which she always called her 'parlour'.

The cats were always the first ones to run to the window when her taxi was not even in sight yet, and I think she always appreciated it when someone was there to welcome her back. She often looked tired when she returned, and her legs were swollen; but she never complained and all she asked for was a whisky to help her to relax.

Christmas was usually spent together at her home. One year, I decided not only to buy a wreath for her door, but also to buy the biggest tree I could find. It was delivered to the door and when it was put up, reached right to the ceiling. I went to John Lewis and splashed out on decorations. She watched me decorate the tree and seemed to be enchanted with the result.

'I never had such a big tree,' she said approvingly.

As always, we had real candles on the tree.

She had made again her special savoury cheese biscuits, and the younger group was busy in her kitchen preparing the mince pies and the Christmas cake according to her grandmother's recipes. I filled up the various decanters, bought some wine and, of course, the turkey which she always preferred to prepare herself.

On Christmas Eve, my son came unexpectedly to say hello, and we invited him and a friend of the group to stay for the meal I was preparing in the kitchen. At midnight, Rina and I went to her local church to attend midnight mass and savoured homemade mince pies when we returned. Her cats were never forgotten: they usually got a treat and perhaps new collars for the occasion.

For her, Christmas was all about giving, and so this time, too, she invited someone from among her friends who might otherwise be on their own to come and join us on Christmas Day. On Boxing Day, the house was open to anyone who had children and wanted to come and visit. She greatly enjoyed being surrounded by young and old when everybody seemed to have a good time, and I always felt that I was storing memories for the future.

Chapter Twenty-Six

In the meantime, my son had started to work at a property company in Mayfair; he had moved out of his father's house and was now living in a ground floor flat in Maida Vale. My daughter, too, had finished her studies and had accepted a job in Hong Kong where she worked as an interior designer.

One day, my son was on the phone and told me:

'There is someone I want you to meet.'

We arranged to meet in Julie's Bar at Clarendon Cross as it was conveniently close for me to get there. He introduced me to his girlfriend who apparently had expressed her wish to meet me. She told me that her parents were Irish, but that she had grown up in Kent. We liked each other from the beginning. I don't know what she thought of me, but I found her not only very pretty, but also intelligent and easy to talk to. As every son's mother knows, it comes always as a bit of a relief when you meet someone for the first time who might turn out to be the future bride, and there is an instant liking on both sides.

After this first phone call, when my son got in touch with me again, I began to see more of the two of them.

Meanwhile, his father was going through another divorce, and perhaps this was the reason why things seemed to have taken a turn in my favour. It was as if my son suddenly wanted to make up for lost time. On many occasions, I was invited to his flat which he shared now with his girlfriend, and together they would prepare a wholesome and tasty meal for the three of us. In summer, they made full use of the back gardens which also contained a tennis court where I joined them sometimes to have a game.

My son had always enjoyed giving people a surprise, and so one afternoon, to my amazement, I was taken by helicopter which, unknown to me, he had learned to fly, to have afternoon tea in a superb rural setting.

After the many years of separation we were finally allowed to get closer again, and our relationship began slowly to recover.

As things continued to progress, we were soon able to celebrate their engagement. I was wearing a two-piece in a pale shade of cream with matching satin shoes on that occasion, and when I finally returned home that evening, I couldn't help being reminded of the young girl who, in her black suit and black satin shoes, had decided to provide a father for the baby she was carrying. A feeling of compassion went out to her, remembering her courage and forbearance, but somehow I also knew that the difficult decision I had to make then had been the right one, and the hardship which I had encountered on the way, was simply an integral part of the path I had been given to pursue. I could see now that the difficult periods in our life, when we learn what suffering really means, always act like a kind of purgatory on us where we are purged and cleansed, and which, like a catalyst, sets the spirit free; in its wake, a fresh start can be initiated, and reality can take on a new and deeper meaning.

From my daughter, too, I received the news that she had met someone in Hong Kong, a young Chinese man from a well-to-do family, but she added:

'We are not in a hurry and will get married when we can immigrate to Canada.'

As it soon became clear, however, we were going to have both weddings the same year, both being, in contrast to my own wedding, lavish affairs; the brides looked stunning and beautiful, the church ceremonies were occasions to be remembered, and the receptions were full of relatives and friends. No money had been spared, and the two couples looked very happy and ready to move on with their lives.

In view of the fact that Hong Kong was going to be reunited with China, my daughter's husband had decided like so many other Chinese to leave Hong Kong and apply for an entry visa in order to immigrate to Vancouver BC in Canada. His mother had already made it her home. A year later, they invited me to visit them. It turned out to be a happy reunion full of memorable moments: I was shown the surrounding areas of the city, and we travelled by car into the mountains where we took the cable car up to the highest point where people came to ski all year round. My daughter and I reconnected and rediscovered how close we were, and I did my best to like and accommodate her newly-wed husband who could be, I should soon discover, quite arrogant. But I tried to ignore this side of him as much as I could and focused more on his brighter attributes.

The same year, my son told me that there was a baby on the way. The flat in Maida Vale would no longer be suitable for a young family. But as it turned out, the paternal home was now vacant. His father had finally decided to give up living in England, to return to his roots and take up his life again in Hong Kong – a move which, I am sure, was the right one for him to make as it offered an altogether more suitable environment for his temperament and lifestyle preferences.

My son was therefore given the go ahead to move into the large house in St. John's Wood for the time being until a more long term solution could be found.

The new baby was a boy with bright blue eyes and blond hair, and I quickly came to enjoy pushing the pram and taking him for a walk when I went to visit them.

At times, I allowed myself to reflect on how things had turned out to be for me, and all the changes which had occurred. I had not only built up a career for myself, but I finally had been given back my family. The children who I had to give up during those long crucial teenage years during their development and who, meanwhile, had found their own partners, became part of my life again, and because they had once been taken away from me, I came to enjoy all the more what I now had.

If I had any regrets at all, it was the fact that because of the long years of my illness and perhaps because of the years of my studies, I was never given the chance to meet someone with whom I could have had a long-term loving relationship. It somehow never happened. I was aware of many a miracle in my life – this, however, was not one of them. But perhaps I had transferred this secret wish of mine to my children, and it was inscribed on their hearts when they began to look for that special person with whom they wanted to spend the rest of their lives together.

On the other hand, my life did not lack in love and affection. I was able to say that although I had lost both my parents when I was in my thirties, I still had a home to go to where I was always treated with the utmost courtesy and caring concern. My every problem, be it with my work or my family, was always freely discussed, and because I trusted Rina, I tended to listen to what she had to say and take her counsel to heart.

Life had taken on a definite shape for me. Its steady course and slow ascent offered me independence, friendship, family bonds, involvement with other people through my work and neighbourhood, and being at peace within myself – all in all a life which was genuine in its aspects, rich in its fibres and creative in its depth. It was a full life and made me feel fully alive.

Chapter Twenty-Seven

My doctor, too, was getting on in years. He had given up his consultation rooms in Devonshire Place and continued to receive only a handful of patients in his home in Kingston. I was one of them.

When his wife to whom he had been very devoted, finally died of a stroke, he employed a housekeeper to look after him and the house. As the housekeeper took one afternoon a week off from her duties, he suggested that I should come and keep him company during those hours when she was out, and he offered to pay me a small sum of money for this service. I accepted his offer as I was glad to give him something in return for the kindness I had always received from him.

That meant that once a week now, I would travel by bus from Central London all the way to Kingston in order to spend the afternoon doing little duties for him like preparing his simple lunch and afternoon tea. He was an old man now, and ate very little, while in the afternoon, he frequently fell asleep in his armchair. But on occasions, old patients still came to ask for his professional help and advice which he was always willing to provide as in his capacity as a doctor, his skills remained undiminished. During these consultations, I stayed in the small television room by the door reading my book.

This arrangement continued right up to the day when I received the news of his death from his housekeeper. He was ninety-one years old when he died in 2005, and had outlived Rina by several years. As at that time, I was booked for another trip to Canada, I was not at his funeral which, in a way, was a blessing in disguise, and I am sure he would have agreed that it was better and more wholesome to be with the living rather than with the dead. But he will never be forgotten.

Chapter Twenty-Eight

Through some strange coincidence, I attended on one occasion an open lecture at The School of Meditation situated in my local High street. Partly out of curiosity and partly out of interest, I listened to what they had to say, and as we were invited to ask questions after the lecture, I asked whether their meditation was purely Buddhist in origin or whether there was also a Christian element to it.

As a result of my question, I was given the telephone number of the Christian Meditation Centre in Campden Hill Road. I had not known of its existence. The call did not take long and I was given an appointment. When I arrived, I was told the simple steps of their meditation. The Centre occupied a beautiful house which had a large and very restful meditation room on the ground floor where one could sit either on a cushion or a comfortable chair. I immediately felt at home in this environment. I was, after all, not a newcomer to meditation though, from Rina's teaching, I knew it only under the name of 'preparation' because you prepared for the day when you sat down in the morning. But the aim of trying to be in touch with your inner self, your innermost being, was the same.

As I had never had any secrets from Rina, I also told her about my experience at the Centre, and, of course, she wanted to know how they meditated and what method they used.

I told her that they used a mantra which was repeated from the beginning of the meditation period to the end, and that an ancient Christian prayer word was recommended as the mantra.

Rina listened very attentively, and when I finished, she said to me very seriously:

'You must practise it regularly for at least six months and then see whether you want to pursue this path.'

I made a start, at first for fifteen minutes only until I was gradually able to lengthen the time to twenty-five or thirty minutes. It took time and effort to sit down every morning, and many were the occasions when I failed to stick to the routine. In these early beginnings, I found that meditation twice a day was simply too much for me. But quite often, I would cycle across Holland Park and take part in the meditation which was held in the Centre every day at noon-time.

Looking back on it now, I feel certain that the encouraging words from Rina were like a last legacy to me; for it was only six months or so later when I called her in the afternoon and heard her say hesitatingly:

'You'd better come. I think I am dying.'

I left immediately and took a taxi to her flat. But I was too late or almost. I found her with her eyes closed, sitting on the floor in a crouching position, next to her telephone and in front of her bed, with her head resting on the edge of the bed. I was overcome with such grief as I had never experienced before; but I managed to take all the necessary steps which had to be made. I rang one of the group members who had been appointed as her executor. I went to call the vicar. And I asked the man next door to help me lift her up onto her bed.

That night, I stayed up nearly all night to keep vigil; but I was not alone; two of her friends, one of which was her faithful cleaning lady, kept me company until I finally retired to what had practically become my room in order to have a short, but restful sleep.

Her funeral was well attended. Many people gathered round her grave while the priest spoke some kind words in memory of her. He mentioned among other things that it was Rina who had shown him through her presence what love really was.

I found comfort in being one among many, but my eyes were dry as I stood at the top of her grave together with her niece. She and her husband had come up from the coast.

After the funeral, everybody went back to her flat where, as she had expressed it in her will, smoked salmon and champagne were served to every friend, relative or newcomer.

In the course of the next few days, I went back to her flat in order to take home a few small items which I wanted to keep as a memento. I sat in her chair and tried to understand that she had left us and that I would never see her again.

My grief and mourning period took many stages where I tried to come to terms with the fact that she was gone. I took refuge in writing poem after poem which remain a testimony to how I felt, and I finished off a bedspread which she had started to crochet for me, but which had been left unfinished.

Yet somehow I also felt that she was still with me. I began to internalize this feeling, and indeed I discovered that she was and always will be a part of me, and that, whatever she had taught me either as a teacher or as a motherly friend, would never leave me and could be relied upon. Eventually, it gave me great pleasure to write down the memories I had, and, as a celebration of her life, I began to bring them to life again in the form of poems.

We as a group still come together twice a year to celebrate Rina's birthday and anniversary, and I am always asked to read some of my poems which seem to recapture her true being in many a way. These get-togethers helped me greatly to share with my friends the sorrow as well as the joy of having known her, as she was and still is an inspiration to us all.

But above all, her death strengthened in me a constant and unflagging need to work on myself in the sense of being; she had set us all a good example: all her life she had remained faithful to her path and vocation, and this was now an incentive for me to follow, in my own small way, in her footsteps.

When therefore the thought of her departure had become somewhat more tolerable, I returned to the Christian Meditation Centre. The pursuit of my spiritual path could begin in earnest, and I was ready for it.

In hindsight, I had been prepared for such a path in various ways. On many occasions I had learned to step back for the sake of the greater good, I had learned to serve without expecting any kind of reward, I had learned not to work for results, and to fit into a community of people who were united by a common aim. Above all, I was shown that the dismantling of those inner barriers which we so easily erect within ourselves, whether they were dissembled voluntarily or, as in my case, removed forcibly through a strong mental and emotional upheaval, opened up new vistas of another reality which had been partly closed to us before. This could lead us back to a new and different kind of normality which is more beneficial and conducive to our true nature and potential.

Under the influence of generous and strong-minded people, people who had a vision in life and who, without any hesitation, looked after me when I needed to be cared for, I was able to learn to trust again and to reshape my life according to new concepts which were greatly affected by their values, their selfless compassion and love; and so my moral beliefs and my faith were rekindled: with their help and guidance I came to believe that despite – or perhaps because of – our struggles and afflictions, we are given to understand that there is another dimension to our life, and if we can allow ourselves to be open to it, it will point us towards the divine. From my own personal experience which I gained along the way, I knew deep in my heart that we are closest to God when we are most vulnerable and in desperate need of his help, and that those of us who do his work here on earth, in this world of ours, will step in to offer assistance and support whenever and wherever they are needed.

Epilogue

In this autobiography, I have recounted all the events as they occurred, as well as the emotional upsets and turmoil which they caused, but I can truly say: everything which happened then rests now in a peaceful and reconciliatory place where loving attention is allowed to be present when dealing with family and friends, and where all distress is summed up in the one prayer: May God bless our failings and shortcomings, and may they be healed by his redeeming love.